Unprecedented Times

Tashawna Thomas Otabil
Visionary Author

Unprecedented Times

ISBN: 9781648589058

Publisher: Trendy Elite Media Group

This book is intended to provide personal growth and leadership strategies that will assist the reader in their journey to developing strong leadership and interpersonal skills. This book is not intended to provide financial, emotional health, or legal advice. Please seek appropriate counsel for financial, emotional health, or legal matters.

Table of Contents

CHERYL STALLWORTH LETT

Foreword Author

Foreword

The year 2020...who could have imagined that a global pandemic would have taken center stage in our everyday lives...forcing us to re-evaluate, reprioritize, and revise every aspect of our existence? Unprecedented times.

One could say that the weeks and months spent in our own homes, restricted from personal contact with others, was an unwanted disruption. But others might say that the time indoors allowed us to realize our own personal development and spiritual growth. But how does one accomplish this? Unprecedented times.

This publication was developed to offer strategies and tactics to survive challenges related to education, relationships, faith, physical and mental health, and finances...resulting from the economic crisis and long-term negative consequences the pandemic has created. The visionary and contributing authors share personal and thought-provoking life stories that offer words of encouragement, coping mechanisms, and tools that afforded them personal triumph navigating this "new normal." Unprecedented times.

One might ask...who are these women? And on what authority are they equipped to offer guidance we should even consider utilizing? Let me assure you that they're an eclectic group of educated, influential, compassionate, and caring women...leaders in our community, managers at billion-dollar corporations, and educators in our classrooms. Couple the professional accolades with their experiences gained serving as a wife, mother, sister, aunt, grandmother, and caregiver...and, you have decades of wisdom enveloped in this shared compilation. I call these women my spiritual sisters, friends, and confidants...and am truly inspired by their stories and life lessons in this book. Find your quiet reading place and enjoy the powerful stories displayed on the ensuing pages. Be blessed!

SHAWNDA JO DERAMUS, MHA

Contributing Author

Introduction:

Unprecedented Times: Strategies We All Need to Survive

The pandemic and social unrest in our society have undoubtedly altered our reality by changing how we interact, the way we view our justice system, and how we create joy in difficult times. COVID19 continues to interrupt our fellowship, finances, health, and wellbeing, which is a challenge. The social justice marches and modest civil liberties advancements continue to be matched by new victims and injustices almost daily. In the early months, perhaps you had a resilient attitude about these developments; however, it is natural to be concerned and somewhat dispirited as it lingers. How long will the pandemic last? How long will our nation continue to turn a deaf ear to the social injustices that plague our society? How do we plan for tomorrow when today holds such uncertainty? That uncertainty in unprecedented times can breed fear; however, we are reminded in II Timothy 1:7 that God has not given us a spirit of fear but of power and of love and of a sound mind! As each of these phenomenal authors has shared, we must claim that power and share that love to survive!

Unprecedented times call for unprecedented strategies! The authors here have shared faith-based and intimate examples of how they have survived and strategies that have allowed them to find joy amid challenges and loss. You most likely found some stories that parallel your life and current struggles. They have challenged you to feed your faith, encouraged you to manage your loneliness, and given you a roadmap to navigate your grief. If we choose to accept it, our collective challenge is to create and share the joy in this uncertainty. Leverage this collection of strategies to elevate your physical and mental health, spiritual wellbeing, finances, and educational pursuits.

As mothers, daughters, wives, and leaders, each of these awesome women have managed to find joy during despair and then shared their testimonies to benefit others. Your task is to reach deep into your spirit to see the steadfast and resolute spirit that resides within. As African Americans, it is imperative that we call upon our creativity, ingenuity, and compassion that is the gift of our ancestors to create a meaningful and impactful life even amid a pandemic and then to encourage others to do the same! We must trust that if God gave us the challenge, then he also has the solution; for that reason, we will have faith. In the words of the old song, "We have come this far by faith and faith will lead us on!"

TASHAWNA THOMAS OTABIL
Visionary Author

True Leaders S.T.A.N.D
(Stop- Take A New Direction)

"A leader is one who knows the way, and
goes the way and shows the way"
– John C. Maxwell

Being a leader can be hard to define during a pandemic but is easily identified. These are the individuals who are willing to lead in challenging environments. They possess characteristics such as confidence, accountability, resiliency and good decision-making abilities. They set the direction and help others do the right things moving forward. Do you have what it takes to **S.T.A.N.D** and lead during unprecedented times? Are you a true leader?

The economic crisis brought by the COVID 19 pandemic exposed vulnerabilities and fragments related to education, faith, finances, racial inequalities, physical and mental health and relationships. While all these challenges created major setbacks, the lack of financial equity has dramatically affected the African American population during this pandemic. Why? Many African Americans have lower-wage positions that were impacted. According to the Pew Research Center survey in April of 2020, 44% of African Americans reported that they or someone in their household had experienced a job or wage loss. Most African Americans don't have financial reserves or savings to cover expenses in the case of an emergency.

True leaders stand out by focusing on how they can take charge of the things they can control. The truth is long-standing systemic financial inequities have set us back for decades. According to an article published by "The Nation," it would take the average African American family 228 years to build a Caucasian family's wealth. African Americans will likely never have equal wealth compare to Caucasians. It will require significant changes in government policies and legislation before different experiences and outcomes are seen. In the meantime, what we can do is take more accountability for our personal finances and spending.

It is not your salary that makes you rich; it is your spending habits.
-Charles A. Jaffe

Stop Take A New Direction (S.T.A.N.D.)

Do you know that African Americans love to spend their money on clothes, shoes, ethnic beauty and grooming products? The Nielson Company reported that 85% of the total US spend for ethnic hair and beauty products are attributed to black consumers. This is the one economic sector that has not been affected by the economy's changes during the pandemic. Simply put, no matter what financial situation currently being faced, African Americans will still spend money on their hair, nails and make-up. The second-highest spending sector among African Americans are name brand fashions. Having the latest pair of Jordan's and expensive purses often reflects a sense of cultural pride with African Americans. However, this must STOP. We must

STOP buying STUFF and start investing our money and establish and create generational wealth.

I recall driving my son to a classmate's birthday party a few years back and as we began driving through the neighborhood, my son said, "Wow, they must really be rich." I laughed and said this is most likely a result of generational wealth. He said, "are we generationally rich?" I said "unfortunately, we are not; when your grandparent and great grandparents passed away, I was left with bills to pay." There was no financial savings. I then explained how important it is to acquire assets and have several savings accounts. I further explained that generational wealth is created when you save money that you don't intend to use when you retire. Those assets and savings are then passed along to your children and grandchildren. Unfortunately, too many African Americans tend to only worry about themselves and the money they want to spend today. They are not focused on the future.

Over ten years ago, I took a financial freedom class course. I learned that many African Americans consistently spend more money than they earn. Several factors contribute to overspending, including easy credit, lack of knowledge, lack of financial discipline and trying to keep up with others. How many credit card offers do you receive via mail or email with 0% interest for 12 months? These are dangerous offers that make overspending easy. Most of the time, we are encouraged by the 0% offers even if we know we can't afford it. We convenience ourselves that we will be able to afford it later because we don't have to pay for the purchase right away. This line of thinking contributes to bad spending habits. We also tend to spend a lot of money on entertainment. Do you give your children a birthday party every year? Do you know how much money the average African American spends on birthday parties? It's nearly $500.00 per child. Stop for a second and ask yourself if your children really need more stuff? What if every year you decided to deposit $500.00 into an interest-bearing money market account for each child, rather than throwing a birthday party? You could possibly have several thousand dollars saved up by the time they reach 18 years of age. Personally, we decided to stop giving our children birthday parties and buying unnecessary Christmas gifts when they were 6 and 2 years of age. We began investing that money into their college saving accounts.

Kids are accustomed to the environment that we create for them. Eliminating parties and gifts didn't hinder our ability to celebrate them. Instead of having a party, we began cooking their favorite meals at home, inviting close family members over and making homemade cakes and cupcakes together. We had to train our family members to stop buying stuff. We simply requested if they wanted to give our children a gift, they could make deposits into their saving accounts or purchase stocks/bonds. I know this sounds dramatic and challenging but the payoff in investing rather than buying stuff that they won't remember 6 months from now is well worth it.

Let's talk about financial discipline. Do you plan how to spend money, or do you just spend it? Do you have a budget and if so, do you follow it? While financial struggles related to African Americans inequality has been on the rise for decades, it is imperative to understand your finances and to keep track of your spending habits. Here are a few tips:

1. Review your current checking and saving accounts and credit cards; Identify spending patterns and habits; Track your spending by categories; Explore using a budget app.

2. Adopt a spending Mantra – Use a cash budget. When the cash is gone, so is your spending.

3. Set Specific Financial Goals – Create a Budget; Follow it; Pay off Debt; Remember small steps equal big results. The debt snowball method strategy. This is where you pay off the debt in order of smallest to largest. In theory, you will begin gaining momentum as you knock out each balance. Instead of focusing on paying extra money on each credit card, you pay the minimum balance. All the extra money should be used to pay off the smallest balance. When the smallest debt is paid in full, you roll the money you were paying on that debt into the next smallest balance. Once all the credit card balances are paid, you can begin building your emergency fund.

4. Build up your emergency fund

5. Save for retirement

6. Start preparing to leave a legacy of wealth behind for your children and grandchildren. Establish

assets and invest in the stock market. Teach your children about the importance of personal finances.

What actions do true leaders need to do to S.T.A.N.D out?

"The most powerful leadership tool you have is your own personal example." – John Wooden

Leadership is a balancing act and it's time to S.T.A.N.D. **Stop, Take, A, New, Direction.** The pandemic brought on challenges that have forced many to stop and take a new direction. Taking small steps with managing your finances will help build your confidence. Understanding that social and economic challenges make it difficult for us to stay ahead, I want to remind you that you are resilient. God will not put more on us than we can handle. Remember, true leaders lead by example and push for greatness by focusing on how they can take charge of the things they can control. You can control your spending. You can teach others how to control their spending. You can make a difference for the next generation. You can create generational wealth. You can S.T.A.N.D. Will you? I pray that this story leaves you feeling encouraged and inspired to S.T.A.N.D.

DELISHA MURRAY

Contributing Author

You Did Not Lose. You Won. -God

While the world was facing a global pandemic, I was facing a personal one. The loss of two parents (my dad and stepmom) in less than a three-week timeframe changed my life forever. All within a moment of time, fear and courage were fighting, depression and happiness were in conflict, and the Spirit of God and the enemy were tugging at my soul. There was a war going on inside of me, and as the days went by, I was losing. I felt defeated, mentally, physically, and emotionally. I did not have the strength to look to God. I was devastated, and a large part of me was deflated. God, why did this happen? Why did you take them now? What will I do without them? We needed them. I had so many questions and a lot of unknowns.

There were days when I felt like I would not make it. I began to pray. I began to pull on every ounce of God in me. I had a wonderful support system, but I needed God. I needed Him like I never had before. Yes, I had gone through trials and tribulations before, but this was different. As I continued to cry out to God—day and night—I slowly began to feel God's reassurance. My prayer time increased dramatically, and I was ready to hear from God. It was then that I began to understand that this was not about what I wanted. God wanted to use this situation for His glory, and He wanted me to share what I had gone through with you. If you have ever gone through a difficult time, I want you to continue to read and find encouragement in some of the lessons that God taught me through the loss of my dad and stepmom.

1. **"God resists the proud but gives grace to the humble..."** James 4:6 (NASB)

As my dad was dying, there was a point in which I felt a sense of entitlement. I felt God owed me. After all, I was pious; I have been faithful in my walk with God, I have treated people right, and I did the right things. Surely, He will keep my dad alive, right? Wrong.

The letter "i" is in the center of "pride." I was allowing myself to entertain a form of pride. Self-centeredness is a form of pride; it is selfish, and it is self-serving. All my emotions were centered on my desires; what I wanted. Yes, I prayed for God's will to be done, but in my heart, I wanted my dad to live, and honestly, I wanted that more than anything. While there is nothing wrong with wanting my dad to live, there is something wrong with the feeling that God owed me.

Lessons:

- God does not owe us anything. His promises are given to us because of our relationship with Jesus Christ. We do not deserve the promises, but only by His grace and mercy.

- When we accept Christ as Lord and Savior, we accept His will for our lives. Always remember that He is in control even through what seems like the uncontrollable.

- Our righteousness is as a filthy rag to God; this means that there is nothing we can "do" in God's eyes that would make us righteous.

- God loves a humble heart, and remember that pride comes before the fall of a man.

2. **For if you forgive others for their transgressions, your heavenly Father will also forgive you.** Matthew 6:14 (NASB)

My dad despised three things; a liar, a thief, and a disrespectful person—he said it all the time, and it has been ingrained in my siblings and me. After he passed, some people close to us lied, stole, and were very disrespectful. It was heart-breaking. I tried my best to pray, but the harder I prayed, the more things happened to make us think that God had forsaken us. One night I was crying out to God when I heard "forgive them." At that moment, I cried harder. I was so angry that I did not think I was going to be able to forgive. I wanted revenge, but I knew I had to forgive them.

Lessons:

- Forgiveness is not for the offender, but it is for you and me. If we forgive others, God will forgive us. It is not optional.

- Forgiveness is a process. Depending on the situation, it can take a lot of time. Be kind to yourself in the process.

- In order to forgive, you must acknowledge that you are in a state of unforgiveness and then *be willing to do* and allow God to do the inner work on your heart.

- Unforgiveness will have us taking matters into our own hands, but vengeance is God's. When we genuinely believe that God is in control and that He has our best interests in mind, we must learn to put things in His hands and leave them there.

3. **A new commandment I give to you, that you love one another, even as I have loved you, that you also love one another.** Jn. 13:34 (NASB)

Days before my stepmom passed away, we had a misunderstanding, and she was upset. I remember talking to her, and I could sense the attitude in her tone. I recall apologizing to her and telling her that I loved her. By the end of that call, I knew that we had made peace. As I processed her death, I could not help but think of all the times I told her that I loved her and how she would respond, "I love you more." In my discouragement, God reminded me that I had done everything that I could to not only tell her that I loved her, but I showed her. Words mean a lot, but words combined with actions truly demonstrate love. This is the kind of love that God requires of us, and this is what He reminded me:

- Love is one of the greatest commandments, and it is demonstrated through word and action.

- We should show and tell loved ones we love them while they are living. Once they die, it does not matter; they cannot see or hear us at that point.

- Never allow anyone to get us to a point where we lose our ability to give love. God loves us so much that He gave us His son. Even in our angry moments or disagreements in life, Godly love should conquer all and cause us to prevail.

- True love, which is demonstrated by actions and words, comes from the heart. It is an inside job. If we have lost the ability to love, we should ask God to change our hearts. He is the only one who can do it.

When you lose loved ones, it is very easy to think of all the things you will miss due to their deaths. However, God had to remind me that I did not lose. I won. Through this process, I won more humility, love, forgiveness—and of course, more of God. If we live long enough, we all will lose many things. However, in our perceived loss, God wants us to focus on Him. Please know that through loss—of any kind, that God has a perfect plan for you. His plan is carefully crafted and created. It includes both grave and great moments, suffering and success, love and loss, death, and destination. However, He is all-powerful, and He always shows us the power of His might when we are going through life's difficulties.

Yes, the journey was challenging, it was trying, but it was not in vain. Whether or not I realized it, things were meant to happen this way. All of us will experience or have already experienced a journey like this. But, as God spoke to me during this, He also speaks to you during your trials. Learn to hear His voice. Learn to accept His plan. Remember that God is with you; He has your front and your back. His love is the most excellent demonstration of love that you will ever experience. Experience Him.

AMBER C. SIMPSON

Contributing Author

An Unprecedented Educational Experience

"History has shown us that courage can be contagious, and hope can take on a life of its own."

--First Lady, Michelle Obama

The Parent as the Teacher

It is often said that the parent is the first teacher of the child. But what do you do when that reality hits during a global pandemic? School abruptly closes, and you are charged with being the direct line for educating your child... This isn't the learning structure we're used to. I don't know how to do this? I'm frustrated! How am I supposed to get my child to focus and learn when I'm working from home?

These are all challenging questions that a parent may ask in this type of situation. This reality also brought about a newfound appreciation for the daily work of educators and schools. Many social media posts and videos of parents acknowledged how challenging it is to get students to focus on learning while eliminating other distractions. It was acceptable for the many hats the teachers wore during a school day while working with over 20 or more students. There were posts of successful at-home learning. Some parents were enjoying the opportunity to teach their children and to support them in creative ways.

We appreciate what is comfortable to us, what we know, and is familiar. When faced with the unknown or unfamiliar, it stretches us and may cause us to pause and seek guidance and wise counsel. In my case, there was a reasonable assumption that a school administrator with over 20 plus years of educational experience would be a pro at remote learning. Admittedly my experience was the exact opposite. I felt the same emotions and frustrations that many parents felt.

There was so much uncertainty, and the transition to remote learning was abrupt and not planned. I love to be proactive and get out in front of things as best I can to prepare. Not being prepared caused me to break down and experience feelings of inadequacy. I am a single parent with the massive responsibility of raising and shaping my child's future and having a tremendous impact on what happens with the 700 plus students that I serve as an elementary school principal. If I felt inept in supporting my child's learning during this time, I can only imagine how other parents were feeling. I began to search deeply inside myself for solutions instead of admiring the problem. I had to speak over and encourage myself so that I could do my job as a parent and operate in my leadership role effectively.

In my time of reflection, I realized that I needed to do three critical things; 1) recognize my weaknesses, 2) focus intentionally on strengthening those areas, 3) find the good and small wins each day, and see the next day as an opportunity for improvement.

During my reflection, I identified areas of weakness related to this remote and professional learning experience. Running the day-to-day operations of a school requires me to juggle many balls in the air. I trust that while my daughter is in her school setting, she is well cared for, nurtured, and getting the academic exposure and enrichment that will lead to successful outcomes. Being in the position to have to run and operate a school remotely did not allow me the comfort to rely solely on others for my child's education during the designated school hours. Our home, known as a place of peace and relaxation, was transitioned into our workspace and serving a dual purpose. Our routine was not thesame.

I also had to acknowledge that I was not fully prepared to accommodate my daughter's specific learning needs while addressing my own. I took for granted the oversight and supervision afforded to her in a classroom setting. Remote learning would require me to be more hands-on with her academics during the day instead of just providing oversight and following up to support healthy communication and relationships with teachers to ensure success. I was going to have to figure out how to keep myself focused and organized in my role as a school leader while also making sure that my child could also follow through with the learning expectations in place during the remote learning period.

Finding Solutions

After identifying and acknowledging my areas of weakness, I began to seek resources and support to address them individually. I started by instituting a student conference time with my daughter. We discussed the changes and began to identify specific tasks to make improvements and adjustments during this time. It was vital for me to hear her thoughts and feelings as well as express my own. This was a time of vulnerability and transparency for both of us. I did not want to drown out her voice because of what I felt as a parent and professional.

These productive and transparent conversations yielded some positive outcomes. We were able to designate separate workspaces for both of us. We set a schedule and expectations for how we would begin our day. We decided to maintain our evening bedtime routine and schedule and set parameters for the workday. We identified comfortable yet presentable loungewear and committed to keeping our routine for getting dressed and prepared for our school and workday. Our workspaces were equipped with the materials and tools that we needed. We were dedicated to specific break times and proper decorum when communicating with each other while participating in class or meeting sessions. I initiated a discussion with her teachers and went over some specifics of her accommodation plan so that they were able to support her remotely while I was making the best effort to adhere to her needs in our home learning environment. I communicated with her teachers weekly and monitored their feedback on the electronic platforms. I was also candid about some of our challenges to provide direct support and reinforcement during their meeting times with my daughter.

These intentional efforts helped me to keep things in perspective and to not focus on my failures. Although this was not ideal, I had to recognize that there were good outcomes every day. Too often, when you are in the midst of a storm, you cannot identify the hurdles that you have overcome or the debris that you were able to bypass because you are so focused on the storm. Finding those triumphs and celebrating the small wins is so significant because it helps us keep going. It also lets us know that even when it looks like it can't be done, there will always be signs to let us know just how possible it is. Even the most minute improvements must be acknowledged and celebrated. We celebrated when my daughter took the initiative and communicated with her teachers without any prompting. If she got out of bed and dressed without me fussing at her or stirring her from a deep sleep, that was most certainly a reason to celebrate. We acknowledged every deadline met, task list completed, and any successful meeting or class session. On the days when things didn't go so well, we still had something to celebrate because each day was better than the day before. We were supporting each other and rooting for our individual and collective success daily. Yes, there were tears and more yelling than I care to admit, but in the end, we were able to get through it by focusing on what was most important, the both of us coming out of this on the other side with more knowledge and a different appreciation for each other.

Reflect and Respond

I share this to encourage others. When faced with adversity or change, it is possible to triumph by identifying and targeting weak areas with focused strategies and support and taking the time to recognize and celebrate the small wins. Hard times will always appear out of nowhere and catch us off guard. When we learn to trust what is already in us and what we can acquire through our connections and relationships, we discover that what we thought was unachievable was just a mental hurdle. Just because it doesn't look the way we want doesn't mean we aren't going to be successful. Don't be so hard on yourself that you miss the blessing. Nothing is so hard that we can't come out victorious or with a positive learned experience. These unprecedented times call for unusual faith and understand that what presents as an impossible challenge is our next elevation.

"Relationships before rigor. Grace before grades. Patience before programs. Love before lessons."
--Brad John

BRANDI SANDERS

Contributing Author

STAY READY, so you never have to GET READY!

COVID 19, unprecedented, pandemic, isolations, quarantine, furlough, layoff, unemployment, family first medical relief act, virtual school, hungry, and budget deficit have become the staple phrase in my new world of COVID 19. As the Human Resources Director for my organization, I am accustomed to policies, procedures, rules, protocols, and consistency. However, this structure went right out the window when we were forced to deal with the everchanging circumstances surrounding this invisible assailant.

March 2020, the entire state was ordered to self-quarantine bringing the City to an abrupt halt, with no clear plan of action. After roughly three weeks, the City found itself in a financial crisis to the tune of a $120 million-dollar deficit and growing. With no real plan, the administration gave the direction to complete an in-depth evaluation of our staff, determine who was essential (needed to deliver service at a minimum leave), and who was non-essential (expendable). We were directed to provide these staff names as soon as possible. As a result of this directive, 1700+ full and part-time employees were selected for furloughed, notified within 24 hours, and release over the next seven days. This was not a simple task, nor was it easy. In fact, the decisions were harsh and emotionally draining. The affected staffs' initial reaction was nothing short of heart-breaking. I lost count after the first 155 calls I received full of fear, worry, and despair. You see, no one was prepared for the just in case something happened, although our country was in a very similar crisis only 12 short years ago; in 2008, when the U.S. economy crashed.

"In the last four weeks, as large sections of the global economy have shut down, more than thirty-three million Americans have filed for unemployment. People with jobs that aren't deemed essential, or that render telework impossible, are suddenly without work, and, in many cases, savings. According to the C.E.O. of Feeding America, the pandemic is likely to leave an additional seventeen million Americans needing food assistance in the next six months." (Griswold, The New Yorker, 2020)

SMACK! March 2020, reality hit many people smack in the face, as they were caught unprepared for the "what if" scenarios that life lunged at the entire world. Astonishingly, it had already been predicted.

"Even before the coronavirus hit, many Americans lived paycheck to paycheck and had little in the way of emergency funds. The personal savings rate had dropped to barely 8% of disposable income, and according to a recent Federal Reserve report, about 40% of Americans would struggle to cover an emergency expense of $400. And a Pew study conducted last month found that just 47% of Americans have enough saved to foot three months of expenses." (Mohan, 2020).

Please note what I tell you next will help you prepare not to be a part of the statistics listed above.

Why have so many members of our culture accepted this systemic form of oppression?

Simple, no one has taught them how to break the generational cycle. Poverty is a mindset feed by a lack of focus and even less determination. We tend to be afraid of the unknown, which makes us unwilling to be bold in our actions or even take risks. As the Human Resources Director for my company, I have personally seen people's lives turned upside down, from the 1700+ employees that were unexpectedly furloughed to the 1000 meals we have served within the communities, every day since the onsite of this pandemic.

Breaking the Cycle

Do not get me wrong everyone could use a helping hand from time to time. However, it is only meant to be a temporary fix or boost at the time. A winning move will be to accept help if it gets you closer to your goal. Nonetheless, when we allow the assistance to become our lifeline is when and where our power is lost. I am here to tell you, do not allow today's circumstances to determine tomorrow's achievements; know there is something greater in store for you.

Steps to transition your mind!

Stop the madness!! Take the wheel, have input on your own destiny, get out of your own way! Stop worrying about what everybody else is doing, saying, or thinks. STOP It!!! Shake that mess off your back, change your lens (your view on your own worth), regroup, get focused. When you are focused, you see the world around you beings to take form; this is where you learn how to make a circle fit into a square. The noise (anything that would distract your focus) will cease, you can clearly see where you want to be, but you have to determine if you are ready to take a chance on you?

Only you can decide.

Step 1: Change your lens?

Take the blinders off (a one-track mind) you needed to broaden your view on life and venture out into the unknown, you have to leap!

Step 2: Learn your worth and accept your truth.

Your very first step is determining that you want more and understand you are bigger and better than your current situation.

Step 3: Set a Goal

Set small reasonable goals. What can you accomplish within the next 6 months that will make you feel good about who you are? Can you pay off a credit card, can you save several hundred dollars, get enrolled in school, take a writing class? Open up a bank account, buy some stock? Remember, a dollar saved is a dollar earned. Whatever you do, do something that will better you.

Step 4: Set a Budget

Set a budget and stick to it. It is important to understand how and where you are spending your money. Ensure that you have listed your savings as one of your bills, and never miss a payment. If your goal is to pay off a credit card or a vehicle once you have achieved your goal, do not stop paying that bill; just change who you are paying it to and pay you.

Step 5: Never give up on you

Do not be fooled, you will get knocked down, you may even get kicked, just keep moving.

Step 6: Get READY, Get S.E.T., G.O.!

BREAK IS OVER! Set a new goal! Plan, prepare, execute. Ask yourself, where do I want to be?

CALL TO ACTION:

1. Your break is over; it's time to BUCK UP, GET UP, WAKE UP!

2. GET READY! Where do you want to end up? How do you need to land? Set a target, set a date. Get a mentor.

3. GET SET! Ask yourself, who, what, how, and why? How did you get here? What do you need to reach the goal (new job, alone time, a fresh start, grace)? Who do you need to meet or align with to help you reach your goal? Why do you want to be there?

4. Go! Let nothing or no one stop you from reaching your goal; you owe it to yourself!

5. Remember, if you stay ready, you will never have to get ready! So are you Ready?????

6. Conclusion

Each of us has a responsibility to hold ourselves and our loved ones accountable. To whom much is given, much is required! Hebrews 4:6, many people entirely misinterpret the meaning of this scripture verse. Must believe, if you have a lot of materialist stuff (money, cars, homes, etc..), you are to be generous and share your riches. However, it is much bigger than that. It truly means whatsoever you have been blessed with, such as; talents, wealth, knowledge, time, and the like, it is expected that we share those things for the betterment of all.

JESSICA FRAZIER, M.ED

Contributing Author

Choosing Faith Over Finances in REST

Max Lucado once stated, "God never said that the journey will be easy, but he did say that the arrival will be worthwhile."

This quote is my story. Fun, fearless, funny, busybody is my makeup. Family Childcare owner by day (bread & butter) and Realtor by night (additional but necessary income) are my career choices. Each day is a new adventure. I rise at 6am (childcare hours 7am-6pm) and conclude between 8pm & 10pm (meetings, home showings, and closings). I absolutely love what I do. I'm excellent at it. People tend to ask, "How do you successfully manage the title of a mom and two careers?" My answer is always, "Only God knows" and his plan isn't always simple & easy." Then I smile, laugh and carry on. My journey has definitely not been easy, but because of faith, it's been extremely worthwhile. In this chapter, I will share my personal story. You'll see that it is possible to remain secure during any struggle in life as long as you choose faith over finances in **REST**. Take a walk with me.

March 26, 2020 altered my world. Realtor life was the same, but my Childcare life shifted. On this day, Ohio Childcare facilities were ordered to close due to the national coronavirus pandemic. Some facilities were able to remain open if granted a temporary pandemic license. Under this short-term license, childcare facilities could remain open to provide services to families in the healthcare and/or safety industry and those considered essential workers. This license was only offered to Childcare Centers (childcare owners/facilities that provide services in a building), not Family Childcare Facilities (childcare owners/facilities that operate within a home). It was later revised so that Family Childcare Facilities could apply for be granted permission to remain open.

Being a Family Childcare facility, I had to make a decision quickly. As a single parent and independent contractor (which meant no unemployment benefits from the shutdown and no 401k/retirement benefits to pull) living check to check, what should I do? Do I qualify for the pandemic license? Are my parents included in the "essential workers" category, and if so, should that take precedence over my family and household's safety? If I apply for the temporary license and receive it, is it fair to my daughter that I risk our safety to continue to receive a paycheck? Or, do I peacefully exercise faith and trust God knowing that HE always has and always will supply my every need?

As anyone can imagine, I was mentally exhausted, in need of rest, a financial breakthrough, and an answer as to what my next move should be. I didn't know that God had a different type of rest in mind for me and that HE would make the decision very clear. That rest was more than sleep. During this time in my life and in the nation, rest meant **REST** (**R**elying, on **E**verlasting **S**tability **T**hru Christ). This **REST** focused on reflection, revamping, revelation, re-evaluating, prioritizing, relaxation and most importantly, relying on God." In this situation, I needed to make a decision that was best for my daughter and myself. During this unprecedented time, I choose faith over finances in **REST**. I realized that I needed to let go of the paycheck and allow God to provide. I needed to be bold and practice the faith that I say I have. I was reminded of *2 Corinthians 5:7 "Walk by faith and not by sight"* if not everyone else I challenge you to never forget what you can conquer in this life because of the God inside of you. As spiritual leader Marianne Williamson once said, *"We lack faith in what exists within us because we lack faith in Who exists within us."* At some point in life, you will be faced with adversity. I challenge you to fear not, to let go, jump into the unknown so that you won't miss what could be the best opportunity of your life. You will never know unless you let go. As Ralph Emerson once said, *"Fear is a great instructor."*

My next move... I turned everything off in my house. I wanted complete silence so that I can clearly hear from God. I grabbed my Bible and thought about something that my pastor always said, "When you open your bible, God opens his mouth." I don't know about you, but I'm faced with adversities every single time, and I blindly open my bible, I'm taken to scripture that relates to my current situation. I blindly opened my Bible. The scripture was *Nehemiah 6:3 "I am doing a great work, and I cannot come down."* As we know, God knows what we need before we even ask. We also know that God's timing is always perfect and that every need will be supplied. That scripture brought tears to my eyes. I realized that I am doing great work providing quality childcare to inner-city families and helping families obtain their homeownership goals. I also realized that God will not allow me to come down unless what I'm doing at the moment is not what he has planned for me. I asked myself, is childcare God's will for my life right now? Do I need to take a break from a business that I've worked so hard to acquire? What will the families do? Who will help the families that I provide care for? How will I take care of my daughter and the piles of bills? How is it even safe for children to stay in childcare facilities during a pandemic but safe for them to stay in school? There I was again mainly focusing on taking care of others while comprising myself. Childcare owners don't have the flexibility that your typical W2 workers have (Flex in/out time, Sick time, PTO, extended vacations) because the services we provide are necessary for parents to make their living. But who protects the childcare facilities? When do I get a break? I realized that it was time to take back my life and make some changes. God saw that I wouldn't make time for myself on my own, so this was my time. I was reminded of a quote from Nicole Sobon. It reads, **"Sometimes the hardest part isn't letting go but starting over."** I stopped worrying and started praying. After intense heavy prayer, REST and reflection, it was decided that my childcare business would remain closed until the childcare order was lifted. Surprisingly, I wasn't a bit worried about my finances. I was reminded that **"Faith sees the invisible, believes the unbelievable, and receives the impossible." (Corrie Ten Boom) My finances would be just fine.**

    The outcome... The life of a childcare owner/operator isn't a simple one that anyone can do. It takes a dedicated, patient, reliable, and honest human being to take on this career, but yet these workers are underpaid, overworked, and underappreciated. Childcare and education in this country are underrated, underpaid, and underappreciated, yet necessary and vital. Most people don't realize this until one is personally or negatively affected. Despite all of this, I still love what I do. During this time, not only have my needs been met, they've been exceeded! I've learned to take time out for the important things in life. I'm taking better care of myself. The unemployment laws were amended to include payments for independent contractors and small businesses. Grants and loans have been offered to small businesses. I've been able to spend much-needed quality time with my daughter. I've received multiple clients from past clients that want to purchase homes.

God is truly great! I firmly believe that I've received all of these blessings because I chose faith over my financial situation. I know family childcare facilities that chose to remain open and received the temporary license only because they wanted and needed a paycheck. However, I still received all that I needed and more without remaining open because I stepped out on faith. I've faced many challenges and adversities. However, because of my faith in God, I stay positive and motivated. My life circumstances have been inhabited with limitations, but I know that I have limitless potential and God never fails. Despite all of these things, when life gets tough, I challenge you not to allow your worldly issues to dictate your next move without consulting God. Instead, activate your faith. *As author Eric Metaxas said, "True faith is not a leap into the dark; it's a leap into the light."* Your current circumstance may seem dark, but there is a reward, a light at the end if you exercise faith.

When faced with adversities in life, I challenge you to step back and **REST.** During your period of **REST,** consider doing the following:

- Remain positive and surround yourself with positive people.

- Pray instead of worrying. Philippians 4:6

- Stay busy making a difference.

- Thank God for things you have, don't focus on what you don't have.

- Be willing to tackle the challenging things in life. Matthew 16:24

- Don't be afraid to start over or take a break.

- Allow Christ to lead you Matthew 11:29

- Self-care is essential. Self-care doesn't mean selfishness.

- Remember that careers and titles come and go, but God remains the same.

Choose faith over your finances and **REST,** knowing that God has your back.

ALMAZ WARE

Contributing Author

The Marriage Marathon

A few years ago, I ran my first 10K. The last mile was by far the hardest. Each time my foot hit the pavement, I felt the highly coveted "runner's high." When I ran across the finish line, I said to my friends, "I have no idea how a human could possibly run a full 25K marathon". And yet, somehow, hundreds of thousands of capable humans around the world accomplish this endeavor. The secret? Resilience.

These unprecedented times have added an interesting route to whatever marathon you are currently running.

Is COVID 19 Changing Relationships?

Chad is a Director at his corporation leading a team of professionals, and I am an Organizational Development and Training Manager. Two "bosses" are now told they must literally merge work and family while coexisting as husband and wife. As we maneuver homeschooling, a screaming baby on conference calls, and of course, wifi issues, we realize we are running through a natural disaster with no sign of relief in sight.

Adversity brings out different sides of people. These sides may have always existed, but now observing from a different angle adds a new layer of intriguing complexity. Being able to quickly adapt is an imperative trait in all facets of life, but especially marriage. Whether it's powering through COVID or simply growing together through the years, optimistic adaptability must be an act of intentionality. Romans 12:2 says, "Do not be conformed to this world but be transformed by the renewing of your mind. Then you will be able to test and approve what God's will is – his good, pleasing, and perfect will." By embracing our ever-evolving environment, we are preparing our lives for resilience. Whether it's working from home in isolation due to a global pandemic, overcoming the heartbreak of losing employment, or even adding a child to an established family - we cannot remain stagnant.

Who am I Married to?

Prior to the pandemic, Chad and I would endlessly text throughout the day. He would respond to my "you will not believe what just happened" messages. I would share my thoughts on his political articles and thought pieces. Now sitting less than 10 feet away from each other, we can simply look over and interrupt the other in the middle of an email to release our thoughts. We now see firsthand how the other unenthusiastically reacts to the other's personal interests and real-time updates.

We must bless our significant other with the space to be different. Ephesians 4:2-3 states, "Be completely humble and gentle; be patient, bearing with one another in love." We must not condemn those we love simply because their interests and opinions differ from our own. Every passion we possess does not need to be equally revered. Each opinion does not need to be adopted or supported. Managing our expectations in our significant others will build our relationship resilience. With that said, simply providing the space isn't enough, but by actively engaging in those interests by asking meaningful questions and being present despite conflicting interests will be an investment in which the return grows tenfold throughout the marathon.

Your Relationship can Survive COVID

God willing, we are nowhere near the finish line of our marriage marathon. This global pandemic is simply a weight we are currently carrying to build our resilience. As we continue to face meaningful moments in our life, we will inevitably evolve, and our environments will shift. We must remember to be adaptable while simultaneously partnering with our significant other to act as change agents as our relationships evolve. We must not miss the opportunity to pour out grace for our significant other like hot water into a bubble bath. This is a precious gift we cannot forget to offer, especially during unprecedented times. Resilience does not exist without tension. Growth does not occur without having something to grow from. Philippians 4:13 states, "I am able to do all things through Him who strengthens me." I pray that we can all remember to put God at the center of ourselves and at the center of our marriage marathon. With Him, we have the secret endurance needed to cross the finish line.

"On your mark. Get set. Go!"

Kasi M. Jordan

Contributing Author

Poverty Does Not Have to Be Your Reality

"You may not control all the events that happen to you, but you can decide not to be reduced by them."
Dr. Maya Angelou

Is Poverty Really A Temporary State?

What is poverty? Merriam-Webster's Dictionary defines poverty as *"the state of one who lacks a usual or socially acceptable amount of money or material possessions."* "Usual" or "socially acceptable" are terms that can be subjective, meaning they are based on one's personal knowledge or experiences. If three people sat down to define them, there would be three different answers. Being poor is a construct that is determined by the environment in which one is in.

For example, nuns take a vow of poverty but are not poor. Their basic needs are met, and the excess items that society lures people to believe they need are entirely ignored by them. While being a nun is an extreme example, it highlights the differences between being poor and living in poverty.

Poor is an economic state, and poverty is a mindset. Shifting a mindset can be the foundation needed to move out of poverty. Holding the belief that better is possible, that goal can be reached, and that wealth, if it is desired, can be obtained, will mentally push you to move. It is not possible to commit to wanting more and not moving forward. If you believe this to be true, then YES, poverty is a temporary state!

Where Do I Start?

"Every time you state what you want or believe, you're the first to hear it. It's a message to both you and others about what you think is possible. Don't put a ceiling on yourself." – Oprah Winfrey

In order to get to one million, you have to begin with one. One step, one dollar, it doesn't matter. Setting funds aside for a rainy day is sometimes like starting that new diet on Monday. It is something many of us push off to some other time, and when that rainy day finally shows up, we have regrets of what we "coulda" and "shoulda" done. Preparing ourselves to be financially stable and independent should not be a daunting task. Because it is an investment in oneself, it should be easy - - but it's not.

Setting out on the path of financial stability can be scary because, for many, it is an area where we have never been. Most people are trying to establish wealth. In a 2019 report by the Credit Suisse Research Institute, only 1% of the world's population currently holds over 44% of household wealth (Investopedia.com), which means many of us are still trying to get to the infamous pot of gold.

Unlike that pot that sits at the end of a rainbow, increasing your personal wealth can be easy to do. Like most things in life, start off by consciously making a plan. Ask yourself, "How much can I afford to save and invest in me?" It is important to acknowledge that you are doing it for yourself, make it personal, and dream big. This will offer some of the motivation and discipline that you need to move forward.

There's an old Swedish proverb that says, "He who buys what he does not need, steals from himself." Remember that nun example from earlier? You have to change your thinking about spending. Be honest with yourself and ask if that purchase is a need or a want. Even if it is a want, be honest with yourself, so you can begin to acknowledge how often you want something. Is it because something upsetting happened, or because you had a little left after this pay period? Lying to yourself about your spending habits will cause you to be stuck in that mindset of poverty.

Another helpful tool that can be used to get you started on your financial freedom journey is a calendar. Using a calendar to write down when bills are due and how much you need to pay on the bill will help you visualize your monthly spending. Are you spending too much each month because of all of that "want spending?" Does your "want spending" double your "need spending?" Be honest with yourself. Ignoring the patterns that you see will only hurt you in the end.

The Next Generation...Our Children

"The greatest gifts you can give your children are the roots of responsibility and the wings of independence." — Denis Waitley, motivational speaker

Being poor and/or living in poverty can be a debilitating feeling that cycles through families for generations. Is it fair for our children to inherit a financial situation that they did not ask for? Any reasonable person would answer, no! After the parent has made a conscious decision to improve their personal finances, here are steps that can be taken to set our children up for success.

> **Step #1**: Talk to them. Don't expect your young adult to understand everything about money, wealth, spending, and saving, because quite honestly, many of us didn't.

> **Step #2**: Add your young adult as an authorized user to any one of your accounts. Your child will automatically inherit your credit score. They do not have to use whatever the line of credit is. There is no easier way to begin to create generational wealth than getting your child set up with a great credit score.

> **Step #3**: Start a savings account for your child. Start them out, understanding the concept of "paying yourself first." Installing this self-discipline practice will pay off in the long run by setting them up for that unavoidable rainy day or for retirement. Having a healthy savings account also creates financial independence.

The above actions are steps any parent can take to get their young adult on a financial stability path. The real-life knowledge that's imparted on the young person will allow them to begin on solid footing. This is how generational wealth blossoms.

My challenge to everyone is simple: break the cycle. Start today to make strides towards financial independence, strides that change your thinking about being stuck in a poverty mindset. It is never too late to repair a low credit score and to foster a stronger financial sense within your children. This next-generation could be afforded a homeownership opportunity at an earlier age, ownership that could then be used as leverage for future business moves. Generation Z is open to taking risks and are willing to venture into entrepreneurialism without hesitation. Parents, mothers, stop holding your children back! Teach them well and let them claim a true inheritance from their parents. Something far more significant than money. Financial knowledge will ensure poverty is never their reality. This does not mean they will always have cash at their fingertips, but it will mean their credit is strong enough to allow them to always have what they need. They will never be poor!

SHEVA STEPHENS

Contributing Author

Vison to Faith: when 20/20 is not so clear

When the term 20/20 is heard, it immediately evokes an idea of clarity. The beginning of the year 2020 did not have a different effect. From Watch Night Services to vision boards, commercial marketing campaigns, and personal conversations. Everyone had a declaration of 2020 being the year of vision for whatever was wanted in people's lives. Coming on the heels of a tumultuous convoluted year of empowerment for women with the #METOO movement, I, like most women, found myself in a place of awe of being heard.

There was nothing unique about most in my space, and I declared my "2020 Vision". I, being a seminary student that had taken a very laissez-faire attitude toward my ministry and education, had announced on January 1, 2020, that I would begin to focus and give God my best. With a dedicated workspace in my home office, a calendar wholly organized, and a family meeting conducted with "buy-in" of support, I was ready to take on 2020. I am sure that I was not alone. And then life began to happen.

Highlight Reel of 2020 Part 1

January 2020 -Kobe Bryant dies a violent death sparking worldwide mourning. President Donald Trump was impeached with what appeared to be evidence that would surely render a change of power in the United States of America. Rumors of a deadly virus headed toward the United States of America. This caused a delay, but not a denial in the Vision 2020 plans.

February 2020 - President Donald Trump is acquitted, and a belief and faith in the American conscience begin to wain. The rumored deadly virus that got a "news crawl" now had a name, and it is COVID-19. This virus is being categorized someplace between a political hoax to unravel and distract from the impending presidential election in the US and reincarnation of an Egyptian plague.

March 2020 - Many US States go into a quarantined state. A position not seen in the US in most people's lifetime. All Major Sports canceled. The economy of the spring and summer comes to a complete halt—stock markets crash. The flow of cash worldwide come to a standstill. Millions of Americans are furloughed from employment, and personal economies and families are in a state of limbo not seen since the stock market crash of the 1930s.

April 2020 - Many people dying as the response to the COVID-19 was varied at best. The most vulnerable of the population of the world is affected. The elderly, immune-compromised individuals, and those with a lack of access to health care become the immediate victims of COVID-19. A spotlight on the disparagement of healthcare access becomes an underlining headline as the US tries to respond to a national pandemic.

May 2020 - The recorded and viral viewing of the death of George Floyd sparks a WORLDWIDE response to the devaluing of the black body. The different reactions of law enforcement to black Americans and white Americans in identical situations. The Black Lives Matter movement is in the headlines once again. Every state in the union had a protesting response to the repeated deaths of black men at police officers' hands in the US. Change is demanded.

June 2020 - America is confronted with its racists' origin and systemic racists' policies that have continued to negate and disproportionately affect the black Americans in America. And the WORLD demands a response. The world demands that the US change.

Let's pause and breathe. It has been a nonstop year that seems a lifetime away from the January 2020 vision. It is this same space that has most questioning all that seems reasonable and empowering. It is almost impossible to even connect with the excitement and fervour that burst into the year 2020. I sat at the beginning of July 2020 and decided to do a mid-year checkup on where I was and honestly cried the kind of cry of loss. Absolutely nothing had been accomplished on my list. All the planning and preparation had meant nothing. I had absolutely nothing to show for 2020.

Ecclesiastes 5:5b says It is better not to vow than to make a vow and not fulfill it. Do not let your mouth lead you into sin[1]. This bible verse echoed in my mind as I looked at my midyear check-up. It was at the depths of this darkness and failure of completion that the voice of

---

[1] "Ecclesiastes 5:5 It Is Better Not to Vow than to Make a Vow and Not Fulfill It.," accessed August 3, 2020,
https://biblehub.com/ecclesiastes/5-5.htm.

God can truly be heard and understood. It is here that I hope to encourage others as I have been inspired.

Vision is defined as the state of being able to see. It is further described as the ability to think about or plan the future with imagination or wisdom[2]. Hebrews 11:1 says, "Now faith is the assurance of things hoped for, the conviction of things not seen." This would be the most concise biblical definition of "faith." The Greek meaning of the word faith indicates a belief or conviction with the complementary idea of trust. Faith is not a mere intellectual stance but a belief that leads to action. Hebrews 11:6 says, "And without faith, it is impossible to please him, for whoever would draw near to God must believe that he exists and that he rewards those who seek him.[3]"

Moving towards the vision through faith

Vision is about seeing, but faith is about trusting. Trusting a process when you can't see. Faith is about trusting that what is happening is for the best and will ultimately render the goal. Faith is about trusting that the journey that you are taking will eventually land you where you believe you are supposed to be.

---

[2] "Vision Definition - Google Search," accessed August 3, 2020, https://www.google.com/search?q=vision+definition&rlz=1C1SQJL_en US859US859&oq=vision&aqs=chrome.5.69i57j0j46l2j0l3j69i65.4926j0j 7&sourceid=chrome&ie=UTF-8.
[3] "What Is a Biblical Definition of Faith?," *CompellingTruth.Org*, accessed August 3, 2020, https://www.compellingtruth.org/definition-of-faith.html.

Trusting the process. Every month of 2020 thus far from one perspective appears to be a complete contrast and distraction from the plan...the vision of 2020. However, faith tells me that each event of 2020 has value towards God's goal for me and your life. Every seeming distraction has a purpose for the culmination of your complete picture. Often, we are so committed to the checklist of life that we negate the destination's journey. 2020 has been full of global occurrences. Each of the events mentioned above forced the world to stop. It is easy to disregard this stoppage as not relevant to me. It is easy to view this stoppage as not relevant to you. However, I would suggest that it is most pertinent at a personal and individual level.

The substance of Faith?

Here is the place for the question. What does it all mean? How does all this relate to my journey and my vision? I am glad you asked.

Our vision is often clouded and predetermined by our desire for what we understand to be a clear path. Our vision is clouded by what we see. What we see is often determined by what we have experienced. Experiences often hinder new conclusions and possible expansions of our sight. But faith allows for God to engage us and encounter things that we would never have participated in. Faith! Trust in the process expands the field of possibilities.

I did not tell you that my path of study is the development of my spiritual formation surrounding the ability to pastor God's people. My vision and calendar were structured around reading required books and journaling about my perspective on what I had read. The "distractions" of 2020 have developed my formation in a way that my calendar could never have.

The global events of 2020 appeared to be a set up from the devil to derail my graduating goal. I could not find time to read or concentrate. I could not find time to focus on the words in the dated books assigned on the syllabus. And then I asked God, why? And as if we were in the movie I, Robot, I heard God say, "Not the correct question." I then asked, "What am I supposed to learn from all this? Is it a distraction or a journey for me to pay attention to?"

Now, my journey may be different from yours; however, you are still on a journey. You have a vision board. You have a checklist. You are possibly aggravated by the occurrences of 2020, or 1998, or 1973. You are discouraged about what you have or have not completed. May I offer you another perspective? Instead of checking your life against your vision, how will your faith be developed to grow you?

What God has told you about your "level up" has not changed. Trust the process to the destination.

BEVERLY ENGRAM

Contributing Author

A Journey of Strength...Not Mine, but God's

They say if you want to make God laugh, make plans. I had plans to retire in 2020 and start a non-profit organization to provide assistance for low-income African-American families to replace their lead water service lines. Oh, but no, God said not so fast, my child. After my annual mammogram, I got a telephone call from the doctor's office stating that my picture wasn't clear, and I needed to get another mammogram. Upon arriving at the mammography area, I saw the image of my left breast on the screen. The image included some white spots that the Radiologist had circled. It was clear to me that something was there. After the mammogram, the technician asked me to get dressed and meet the Radiologist in the office. Oh wow, I'd been getting regular mammograms; this was not the normal process. The Radiologist explained that there were micro-calcifications shown on my mammogram.

While this is common in women over age 55, and only 15% are positive, I needed a biopsy to be sure. It was around Christmas time, and I didn't want to alarm my family and close friends, but I knew in my spirit that I was one of the 15%. The call came on January 7, 2020, "Mrs. Engram, this is Mary, your biopsy came back positive, and you will need to meet with a surgeon to discuss next steps." A telephone call, then ensuing a journey that no woman wants to take. I was diagnosed with Carcinoma in Situ or a non-invasive type of cancer, Hormone Receptive positive (HR+). As the surgeon, oncologist, and

Radiologist stated, I had the "good" type of cancer—but I said to myself, "what, cancer is cancer, what's the good type? Stage 0, detected very early, but I was normally a healthy person. I can't have cancer. Okay, I got this!" The surgeon was reassuring and let me know that she needed to remove the abnormal cells, and since it was caught early, there was a 90% chance that I would beat this situation, and this stage of cancer was not life-altering or ending. As a precaution and to ensure the abnormal cells did not return, I would need to take radiation treatments and the 5-year pill.

I recovered from 2 surgeries, and just when I was gaining control over my life, this Pandemic called the Coronavirus was confirmed in the United States. The Coronavirus reported cases in the United States began to grow, including confirmed cases in Ohio and the Cincinnati, Hamilton County area. The Governor declared a statewide "Stay at Home Order," and we were sheltering in place. Oh, my God. My world came to a screeching halt. How would I go through this life-changing process alone? My mental health requires me to be around other people.

The first order of business, I canceled my scheduled retirement. With the stay at home order in place, I couldn't travel, where was I going anyway? I had to complete 16 daily radiation treatments. The Coronavirus and stay at home order required that I work from home. I was actually okay for the first month. After that, I began to feel isolated and lonely. John Donne's "No man is an island" quote is so accurate. I quickly became bored with the daily routine. God did not intend for me to be alone.

He intended for me to be with people. I am at my best when I can see and be around other people. I used technology to fill the void of physical or face-to-face contact with people. Instead of sending text messages, I actually made calls to others. It was great to hear someone else's voice, to listen to them laugh, and hear the smile in their voice. FaceTime calls were a great way to talk and see our family and friends.

We are all leaders, creative thinkers, and regularly address change at our jobs. I just needed to call upon my strengths and make the best out of my new normal. The stay at home order was a blessing in disguise and an opportunity for me to be creative and use the time working from home to my advantage. This is how my life would be during retirement. I would volunteer as needed, and since all my friends and family still worked during the day, I would need to be creative to occupy my time.

I started the 16 rounds of radiation treatment. Fatigue was a side effect of the radiation treatments. Insomnia, depression, loss of bone density were side effects of 5-year medicine. To help counter the side effects, I began to walk/run for 30 minutes each day. According to the Mayo Clinic, a brisk walk can help maintain a healthy weight, manage heart disease, type 2 diabetes, and strengthen the bones and muscles. I have completed over twelve half marathons, and I enjoy being outside. Working from home allowed me to make time to go out or on the treadmill every day. The walks/runs helped in several areas. And I planted a garden. Gardening was a very good way of getting daily exercise and keeping my mind sharp. Maintaining the garden was a lot of work, and I enjoyed going out each morning to water and see the vegetables growing in the garden.

Through all of this, I knew that I had a greater purpose. I knew that God wanted me to share this journey with you. I have outlined some of my learnings from all of this and hope that it will encourage you.

1. Don't ignore the empty feeling: Let's be honest, the feeling of emptiness and loneliness from being isolated can take a toll on the mind. Isolation opens us up to attacks on our spirituality, depression, and I was becoming angry. The first step in healing is admitting there is a problem. Don't suffer in silence.

2. Seek counseling: A very wise woman advised me to utilize the professional counseling available through my employer. If counseling is not available through your place of employment, it is an excellent investment in your health and well-being. She also suggested using the time to talk only about yourself and your feelings.

3. Do something: Since you're in the house during the Pandemic, it's time to do some things that you've thought about doing, like writing a book. LOL. Keep your mind occupied by reading books, crafting, and completing puzzles.

4. Stay social: Wearing masks is important to reducing the virus's spread and became mandatory by the state. My friends and I took on

a community service project. We met one day a week and made masks. We also had socially distanced driveway happy hours where we played trivia and other games.

5. Stay healthy: This is not the time to skip doctor's visits. During the Pandemic, I completed 16 rounds of radiation and kept several doctor's appointments as part of my new normal. My doctor's visits were easy. Other than the radiation treatments, the appointments were virtual and timely. No more crowded waiting rooms and unnecessary time spent in the doctor's office. I had to make my health a priority.

6. Beat cancer: Please know that we can beat Breast Cancer. Breast Cancer is not a death sentence. Get your annual mammogram each year. If you have dense breast tissue, get the 3-D imaging instead of the general mammography test. My cells would not have been detected using general mammography. The cancer scare, along with the Coronavirus and Pandemic, was difficult for me, but with God's grace and mercy, I have learned to appreciate my family and friends and focus on the important things in life.

7. Have faith: During this process, my faith was strengthened, and it was easy to attend live streaming church services and bible study. This time inside allowed for introspection.

8. Self-awareness is key: Dig deep within yourself and really become self-aware. Learn a new skill,

overcome a weakness, or work on some areas that strengthen and make you feel good.

9. Practice self-care: Take care of yourself, physically and mentally. How can you be a blessing to others if you don't take care of yourself first? Life is precious, don't sweat the small stuff.

10. Be intentional: Focus on the important people and things in your life that bring you joy and allow you to be a positive influence on other people. Reach out to others and support them; they may be feeling the same about being isolated. Together you can work through any situation. Cancer tried to attack my body. Isolation during the Pandemic tried to attack my mind, but the love of God, my family, and friends helped me through it all.

Through my cancer journey and this Pandemic, I remember that I can do all things through Christ who gives me strength. I leaned in on Him, and I want you to be encouraged to do the same.

TIFFANEY LIVINGSTON HARDY

Contributing Author

Joyful, Joyful!

"Our deepest fear is not that we are inadequate. Our deepest fear is that we are powerful beyond measure. It is our light, not our darkness that most frightens us. And as we let our own light shine, we unconsciously give other people permission to do the same. As we are liberated from our own fear, our presence automatically liberates others." — Marianne Williamson and echoed by Nelson Mandela in his 1999 release from prison.

Anyone who knows me well knows that I truly aspire to shine the light of God wherever I go. We are all created to share and reflect God's light. My parents and the village that raised me in the foothills of Johnson City, Tennessee, taught me to always love and be considerate of others. For me, one of the greatest gifts is love and the gift of hospitality, but sometimes it can leave one's heart heavy and unguarded. When you are the one always cheering others on, the question becomes, who cheers for you? Who cheers you on?

Someone asked a random question on social media that immediately got my attention. It was a rather simple question, asking, "how are you doing"? The person who posted it wasn't simply asking a flippant question, but he sincerely wanted to know how people in his circle were doing. I pondered the question throughout the day. My thoughts surrounding the question surprised me, and I had to afford myself the grace to not be okay.

The grief my family has experienced since 2017 seems insurmountable and sometimes too heavy of a burden to carry. In the three previous years, I have lost two brothers-in-law James Grove and Chollie, and my sister-in-law Jeanie who lost her heroic battle to cancer. Between 2018-2019 alone, I lost my husband, my son's godfather, my amazing father, my Uncle Bear, my cousin Kenneth who was murdered in Chicago, and my beautiful MeMe, a grandmother me and great-grandmother to my son. That same year my beautiful niece Addie Lee (named after my grandmother!) lost her beautiful mother Jennifer and her great grandmother and great grandfather – all in one year and before the age of five.

So, the day my grief turned to anger, it really surprised me. We all know the five stages of grief: denial, anger, bargaining, depression, and acceptance, but it hits different when you don't quite recognize the person looking back at you in the mirror. This is especially true after one of those ugly cries. These five arbitrary stages are ways in which people can navigate through the world of uncertainty and learn to live again after losing their loved ones. It is a way to process the assorted waves of emotions not through some prescribed linear way of grieving but through the waves of life that ebb and flow within our ocean of grief.

"Fear Doesn't Stop Death, Fear Stops Life"
David Kessler

I had experienced many of the five stages of grief, but anger had not been one I had dealt with to this point. So why the anger and why now? Why was I afraid to explore the anger that I was currently feeling? It was one late Friday evening after a busy work five months into the COVID19 pandemic. I was emotionally spent after a traumatic experience with a contractor I hired to perform some work. The contract was not executed as planned, and police officers were called in to offer assistance. My son and I, and several friends, were personally affronted, and that's where the spiral began that night. Unknowingly that staircase of grief appeared almost out of nowhere merely from a business deal gone wrong and quickly led me down a dark, narrow path straight to anger. I was angry, simply angry. I had become angry that my loved ones weren't there, that my niece's mother was no longer there, that my father wasn't there, and most importantly, that my son's father wasn't there.

The anger made me feel afraid on the one hand, but it did bring about a rawness that I very much needed. What I learned is that anger, if managed carefully, can actually be helpful, bringing about a sense of connection to oneself and others. The anger might present itself in feelings of "why me" or "life isn't fair," but it can bring about much-needed healing if explored. I recently read that while anger is generally frowned upon in our society, it is vital to open the door of anger and walk through it, even if it seems too hard to bear. It is essential to feel it – all of it. Sometimes, the more you allow yourself to feel and deal with the anger, the quicker it may go away. After the anger and acceptance, where do you go, and what comes next? In his book, "Finding Meaning: The Sixth Stage of Grief, David Kessler argues, "it's finding meaning beyond the [five] stages of grief most of us are familiar with that can transform grief into a more peaceful and hopeful experience, or a new meaning in one's life." Finding meaning is ultimately the gear that shifts us to the next level allowing us to get back to our joy.

"...for the Joy of the Lord is my strength!" –
Nehemiah 8:10

Learning to navigate through this COVID19 pandemic and subsequent quarantine has been particularly challenging for most. There has been so much loss, sickness, death, uncertainty best characterized as Corona grief. In a moment of unbelief, imagine my complete shock when I tested positive for COVID19. I was scared, disappointed, hurt, and I absolutely feared the worse. After all the precautions I had taken wearing masks, handwashing, social distancing, and working from home, I somehow contracted this unknown, deadly disease.

Simply put, I was afraid and just as frightened sharing it now. I told very few people and fully isolated during this time. It was absolutely the loneliest and scariest times of my life. Thankfully, I was asymptomatic only with minor symptoms. Even though I went through this unfortunate COVID19 journey, I count it all joy as I learned so many things: that God is my protector and healer, that God and the universe will send people in your life to help you through life's trials, that in Him I am more than enough, to rest and find rest in Him, to be grateful for all things big and small, and to trust Him and put my trust in Him. For the first time in my life, I truly felt the joy of the Lord for it all – His love, healing, strength, presence, protection, provision, grace, and salvation.

> *"For me, becoming isn't about arriving somewhere or achieving a certain aim. Instead, I see it as forwarding motion, a means of evolving, a way to reach continuously toward a better self. The journey doesn't end." – Former first lady Michelle Obama, Becoming*

With so much happening in the world, navigating alone through unprecedented times is not for the faint of heart, but as mentioned in Ecclesiastes 9:11, "The race is not given to the swift nor the strong but he who endures until the end." As a woman living through unprecedented times requires the realization that we must begin taking care of ourselves, especially our mental health, from a position of humility. Being humble and understanding that sometimes putting our masks on before helping others is not cowardly, but necessary. As women, we are often told to be brave, resilient, brilliant, and strong, but sis, let that go - really let it go. Being focused and determined is okay but having unrealistic expectations is a set up for failure.

It is okay to NOT be okay. Really, it is. Growth and healing occur with the simple act of accepting where we are on this journey that we call life in order to move forward. And when we need it, sometimes we just need to have a really good, ugly snot cry (like Viola Davis in most of her movies and tv shows)!

Key things to remember for finding hope and new meaning in your life during challenging times:

- Be truthful and transparent with yourself
- Be present with yourself and others
- Provide grace to grow through
- Seek professional counseling
- Reach out to your support system for a listening ear
- Ride the waves of grief
- Ask for help when you need it
- Find something that brings you joy
- Make time for yourself
- Volunteer or give to others

Sis, it's okay to ask for help. It is okay to kick our heels off, take a break, remove our masks, and show our most authentic selves in the comfort of our inner circle. In this process of becoming, we truly learn to love, accept, and value ourselves for who we really are.

LEAH STEWART

Contributing Author

Women and Higher Education
Opportunities and Challenges

Philosophical View on Education

College is an option for all, meaning college should be available to every individual interested in pursuing a formal or advanced college education beyond high school. As a college administrator of over 30 years, that has been at the core of my philosophical views on education and the premise of my personal, professional, purpose, and passion in life. It influenced my personal, educational journey and guided my decision to dedicate my life to a career in higher education. It positively impacted my outlook and approach to students and parents as I play a role in shaping and changing lives. You see, I also understand that a college degree not only changes the student who earned the degree, but it also changes everyone connected to the student – it is a generational change agent.

Now that I have shared my philosophical view on education, I also want to share the reality as I view it. Conversely, I realize that college is not for everyone. Some may even go a step further and say, college is only for the "haves" and not for the "have nots" – it's for the "advantaged" and not the "disadvantaged." Some may even say for males versus females. Throughout my career working on many college campuses, I witnessed first-hand the great divide and inequities when interacting with many students and families challenged with being ill-prepared financially and underprepared academically for college. Navigating university policies, practices, and rules.

I have included an addendum to my philosophical view on education to encompass, based on my personal views and the reality as I see it. I understand that barriers and inequities prohibit students from attending colleges and universities and pursuing their educational endeavors. For that reason, there must be viable alternatives for people who decide to take a different route. Furthermore, I feel that alternative routes should lead to opportunities that support optimum job security, job satisfaction, and ultimately lead people to a successful and rewarding life-long career. Having such alternatives in place offers people the ability to positively contribute to their communities and society-at-large. Let us not forget our history, for it was not until the mid-1820s and early 1830 when Blacks and women were even first admitted into colleges and universities.

Education - COVID-19 – Challenges and Opportunities

I mentioned barriers and inequalities in education, but I did not mention the challenges of life – our history, the economy, or national disasters, all of which impacted our educational systems. Throughout my higher education journey at a large research 1 university, a small private university, and currently a medium-sized 4-yr comprehensive university, I have navigated, endured, and concurred many challenges. I worked through the 1980s collapse of home loans, leading into the 1990s recession, the 2001 Cincinnati riots, 9/11 terrorist attacks, school shootings, to name some, and now, Coronavirus (COVID-19).

COVID-19 is a national pandemic that came in like a quiet storm and continues to roar like a lion. Just as many other challenges, it has affected our Black and Brown communities horrifically, that further elucidates the historical systematic, and institutional disparities. Black Americans are contracting and dying from the Coronavirus much higher than their representation across many states. Those at the bottom of the US's financial brackets will most likely be affected by the crisis. Another tragedy is that Black Americans are more likely to have underlying medical conditions such as asthma, hypertension, diabetes, and heart disease, putting us at high-risk and vulnerable COVID-19. Interrelated inequalities spill into education. Simultaneously we are experiencing declining high school completion rates and barriers to college retention rates during the pandemic.

As many schools transformed to providing virtual educational opportunities, many home environments were not prepared or adequately equipped to handle at-home learning for children and adult learners. Women were faced with even greater challenges, not just health and employment challenges; we are also more likely to be presented with day-care challenges and much more due to the pandemic. We are more likely to be single heads of households than white women. So, we find ourselves balancing competing demands of work, online distance learning, and child-care responsibilities.

When examining education disparities and socioeconomic gaps, let us not forget our history, for it was not until the mid-1820s and the early 1830s when Blacks and women were first admitted into colleges and universities. We also must understand that in our recent history, the late 1960s, most African-American, Latino, and Native American students were educated in segregated schools where funding rates were lower than those serving whites. It wasn't until 1970 when efforts to equalize spending tried to make a difference in the student achievement gap. Our history is important because it paved the way for the current and future opportunities for many and, in particular, for Black women.

I believe that when Black women began to believe that education is a key pathway to social mobility, they were also able to understand the value, importance, and worth of higher education. But equally important, colleges and universities have been challenged with providing equal access and opportunities to women. Higher education can serve as an engine for individual opportunity and social innovation. It is an investment for women to foster social change. Education also provides women with entry into male-dominated professions – opening opportunities to shrink the economic gap.

Take Action – Take Charge

While we are dealing with COVID-19, I think it is critical to use this time of disruption to reset our priorities and evaluate and assess our current status while developing future plans. This is the time for meditation and reflection; time for reinventing and rebuilding. It is time to do the work! Women are encouraged to identify and use resources to support them on their new journey. In some cases, this may mean baby steps, while it's a giant leap in other cases. It's customized to your journey and faith walk, as well as your situation. The end goal may be to earn your GED, enroll in college, or complete a micro-credential. But, in all cases, it's self-improvement and propelling you to the next level.

From my work experiences, sometimes, the barriers are small and simple. Black women may not be aware or realize college as an opportunity. Some do not understand how they can afford college, while sadly, others do not understand the benefits. My colleagues would refer to that as the return on investment (ROI) of attending college. There are tons of articles and research on the topic: ROI of attending college. One of the more sensitive issues associated with going to college is financing college. The conversation can get a bit dicey, especially when student loans are part of the equation – it can be a challenge to explain and comprehend. But, in the end, they usually understand the big picture, ROI.

My Passion – My Commitment – My Service

I do not want to paint the picture that everything is rosy or that college is the solution to everything; it is not. For some people, it is not part of their life's journey, never will be, and probably should not be. You see, you have to want it, you have to attend college for the right reasons, and you have to do it for you (no one else, not for parents or friends). When all of those factors align, students typically enjoy their college experience. They thrive and reach their destiny in earning their degree.

I like to view the college journey like any other goal that you set out to achieve. You have to be strategic, plan, and execute. You need to understand your strengths and weaknesses. You need to be aware of the resources that are available for you. You need to not be afraid to take calculated risks and understand that failing is part of your success story. You need to have grit. Grit enables you to cross the finish line and earn your degree. You need to understand that attending college is an option for all, meaning college should be available to every individual interested in pursuing a formal or advanced college education beyond high school.

IVORY PATTERSON

Contributing Author

Father Are You Listening?

"I talk to God, but the Sky is Empty"
—Sylvia Plath.

Have you ever prayed and felt they were falling on deaf ears? Like you were just crying out but into an empty abyss? There are times when the pain and circumstances in our lives make it hard to trust God. Over 200,000 have died from the Coronavirus, and the number of cases worsens each day. So, where is God? Weighed down by my own doubts, I began to explore these feelings more deeply. So perhaps you are like me; you are tired of praying to that empty space in the sky. Do not lose hope—keep reading.

We all experience doubts. These doubts surface in our relationships, careers, studies, and just about every aspect of life. Traditionally, showing a lack of faith or expressing doubts are considered taboo and blasphemous. If you grew up in the church, some seasoned saints might have told you to "just pray harder" or "just hold on." While there is nothing wrong with steadfast and unmovable faith, what do we do when our monotonous Sunday morning routines are no longer enough. How do we cope with unbelief? Mark 9:23-25 tells of a man whose child was ill, and he cried out to Jesus, "I do believe, help my unbelief." Perhaps, like this man, we cope with a lack of faith by asking God for help. God is big enough to handle our doubts and fears regarding our faith. When God said to cast all your cares on him, he meant just that.

Also, Communication is an essential part of any relationship, including your relationship with God. So, when you experience moments of doubt—tell him. Ask him to help your unbelief, and he will do just that.

Grace Under Fire

Ernst Hemingway once said, "Courage is grace under pressure." During these difficult times, many people wonder how healthcare workers have the courage to provide care to those diagnosed with COVID-19. The answer is by exhibiting grace under pressure. This was a characteristic I embodied and relied upon heavily during the early days of quarantine. Yet, as millions lost their jobs, fell ill, and grappled with other unfortunate consequences of the Coronavirus, there was food on my table, and my bills were paid. I was stumped—see, I struggled with my doubts for so long, they turned into complaints about God and everything he had not done for me. At that moment, I realized that I literally could not complain because he met and exceeded all my needs.

Think about all the things and activities you participated in before the shutdown. Now think of how many of those things were essential during the quarantine. God never promised us an easy life—but he promised to be with us and supply every need. If He has supplied your essential needs, this is evidence that He is real and cares for you.

As mentioned above, "Courage is grace under pressure." This is an amazing character trait. In fact, Deuteronomy 31:6 tells us, Be strong and of good courage, fear not, nor be afraid of them: for the LORD thy God, he is that doth go with thee; he will not fail thee, nor forsake thee." Though it is written here in black and white, trusting God is no easy task. You may ask yourself; how do I trust someone I cannot see, touch, or feel? From a young age, we learned by looking, listening, and feeling. Faith is the exact opposite of this. Faith is "the substance of things hoped for, the evidence of things unseen (Hebrews 11:1)." It seems that to trust God, we must have the courage to step out on this faith. We must know he is there even when we cannot feel him.

The amazing thing about Hebrews 11:1 is that it mentions *evidence.* Take a moment and think on this word. What evidence is there in your life, and during these difficult times, that God is real? The best way to see God's work evidenced in your life and resist the urge to complain to all five of your followers on Twitter is to practice gratitude. Try writing down at least three things that that you are grateful for. It is so easy to focus on the negative situations that arise in our lives that we develop a bias against the positive. Gratitude is the greatest weapon you can have against a lack of faith. Retrain your mind and heart by creating a gratitude journal—watch your faith begin to shift.

Endure to the end

Perhaps the most misquoted scripture is, "For the race is not given to the swift, but he who endures to the end." Somebody made this up. However, our walk with God will take endurance. There may always be moments of doubt—though I am writing this chapter, there are still days when I slip into old thought patterns and begin to doubt God all over again. Thank God he does not expect us to be perfect! It is in these moments where we should practice self-compassion and give ourselves *grace*. Self-compassion is the practice of being kind to yourself, forgiving yourself. It is when you no longer "should" on yourself. Instead, shift your mindset to understanding that it is okay to feel this way. When these feelings pop up again, as they sometimes will remind yourself of all the ways God has shown up for you. As with anything else, take your faith walk one day at a time.

Steps to Achieve Unprecedented Faith

Unprecedented times call for unprecedented faith. There is no doubt that the current public health crisis has led to several unfortunate circumstances. With no cure and no vaccine in sight, faith is our greatest defense. While achieving this unprecedented faith is not easy, there are very simple steps, just take a P.A.G.E. out of my book:

> **P-atience**
> **A-dmittance**
> **G-ratitude**
> **E-vidence**

Patience—have patience with yourself as you build your relationship with God. Like any relationship, this will take time. Be gentle with yourself as you build your trust in God. You may not be ready for church every Sunday, choir rehearsal every Tuesday, and the Bible twice on Wednesday. No worries. Find what works for you. Many churches have opted for virtual worship experiences, so this may be a good time to court a few different churches. Try streaming a different service each week until you find one you might want to join. If you currently have a church home—still, try other services to be sure you are getting the messages you need for this season of your life.

Admittance—admit to God your struggles with your faith. Get specific, why do you feel you have these doubts? Was there a particular situation that made you begin to experience these doubts? Remember, God cares for you, so remember to cast your cares on him; he can handle it.

Gratitude—you better get you a journal! Write down the things you are grateful for each day. These things do not have to be only material—life and breath are a blessing, peace of mind is a blessing, joy is a blessing. Be sure to capture these intangible things as well. In addition to what you are grateful for, be sure to capture positive things that happened throughout the day. This can be a compliment from a co-worker or friend. If it made you smile, write it down,

Evidence—search for the evidence of God working on your behalf. Whether this is readily apparent to you or if you have to pretend you are in your favorite episode of CSI, take stock of your life and notice the ways that God has kept you, provided for you, and protected you. If you search for it, you will find it.

I challenge those struggling in their faith to try at least one of the activities above for 28 days. This can be in the form of a prayer journal, committing to praying each morning or taking a moment to pause and reflect during the day. After taking a P.A.G.E out of my book, it is my sincere hope that you will experience a shift, and your faith will begin to increase. Be encouraged.

SHERRY WHITLOCK

Contributing Author

Survival By Grace: Marriage, Family, and a Pandemic

The 2020 Coronavirus pandemic has been a life-changing experience for me. See, I easily get bored, and, hence, I tend to stay busy. Before the pandemic, I ran three companies, sat on two non-profit Boards, and was a member of three different volunteer/social groups. While running a household, raising two boys, making sure homework was done, preparing dinner each night, and taking care of my handsome husband. And in addition to all of that chaos, I am a very impatient person who has high blood pressure and strives for order. I like things to be done a certain way, and I love a clean and organized home where everything is always in place. That is just me, and that is how I have operated for years. I never slowed down long enough to truly enjoy the things or the people around me. But, when Coronavirus infiltrated my life and literally shut everything down, I realized that my drive for success and perfection put unnecessary stress on me mentally and physically.

Striving for Perfection

I firmly believe that everything in our lives is strategic. And that the ups and downs are by design. And although Coronavirus has had a devastating impact on everyone's life in one way or another, it has also given many of us wake up calls. For me, it was the realization that I was over-extending myself. I rarely said no when someone would ask for my time or service. And as a result, I was committing to too many activities and neglecting my family and myself. My youngest child is very intelligent, but he has Attention Deficit Disorder (ADD) and was not doing as well as he should have been in school. And without the "wake up call" of Covid-19, my husband and I would have never slowed down long enough to realize that he needed educational assistance at home, in addition to what he was receiving at school. Discovering this gap brought us both to tears. My oldest son graduated from high school this year. And as I was maintaining my Super Woman status, I was also managing his life to ensure that he was on track to finish high school with the expected GPA. Confirming that he submitted college applications, financial aid documents, and scholarship applications on time, making sure that he achieved acceptable ACT/SAT scores, and coordinating college campus visits.

And although the businesses were doing well, it was at a cost. The number of blood pressure medications I take increased, other medical conditions were being called into question, my physical appearance was altering, and the stress of it all was beginning to manifest in my behavior. I had become more irritable and was easily annoyed by the most minute issues.

The Call to Slow Down

Covid-19 has taught me to put my family and me first. My husband has been telling me for years that I need to relax. His favorite line is, "Everything doesn't have to be done today, Sherry!" But, in my mind, I believed that if I get it done today, I can rest tomorrow.

But the problem with that mindset is that tomorrow never comes. I recall the first few weeks of the Coronavirus shutdown feeling like a vacation. I was not consumed with work responsibilities. No conference calls and no customers were calling with complaints or requests. After the first few days of this new life, I could feel the everyday stress and anxiety, leaving my body and being replaced with gratitude and content. I was no longer complaining to my husband or the boys about shoes not being placed in the closet. Nor was I concerned about the kitchen countertop being covered with bread crumbs and jelly. My blood pressure was decreasing, my mind was at rest, and I was rediscovering my family.

The family was excited to be together, and my boys especially enjoyed having their father home. My husband works 12-14 hours per day, so we rarely get to spend a lot of time together during the week. The Coronavirus shutdown has allowed us to engage in activities that we have not done in years. We binge-watched movies and television shows, played games, and assembled puzzles. And just like a lot of other families, we are taking advantage of the opportunity to break bread together every day. My husband and the boys took turns preparing meals (and they actually cleaned up after themselves when done). The boys got creative and started seeking out new recipes to try. A few of the dishes were complete misses. But the majority were really good. The Hot Cheetos Chicken was a miss. But, you have got to try a Shrimp Po' Boy recipe...absolutely delicious!!

Just What We Needed

Listening to Ohio Governor Mike DeWine as he gave details of the pending quarantine had us speechless and unsure of our immediate future. It is well known that the act of being quarantined with others can either improve a relationship or destroy it. Every issue about or dislike you have for the other person(s) will be intensified during this time. And fortunately for us, we realized that we still liked each other after all these years. I am sure our story was a common occurrence during the Coronavirus pandemic. But, I believe three things allowed us to come through this with our family and marriage intact and stronger.

1. Belief in a higher power – Believing in something or someone that brings peace into one's life is amazing. Whether your God is a person, nature, or an inanimate object, we all seek something that will bring about calmness and put our minds and hearts at rest. Find a space where you can mentally remove yourself from the pending problem or situation. And allow yourself time to think and talk through what is going on around you and in your life.

2. An open heart and mind – Interacting with people who ascribe to a positive aura and positive thinking is one of the best situations in which to find yourself. When people respond or react encouragingly, it changes the energy in a room and puts others at ease. Remember, your thoughts become your reality.

3. Adequate emergency fund – An emergency fund is a readily available source of cash to get one through financial hardships such as unemployment, a serious illness, a major repair to your home or car, or a national crisis such as the Coronavirus pandemic. Financial experts state that an emergency fund should contain enough money to cover all expenses for three and six months. Also, know that financial institutions do not offer "emergency fund" accounts. The onus falls on individuals to set up an account and label it for this purpose.

"True love doesn't happen by accident. It's deliberate, it's intentional, it's purposeful, and in the end, it's worth it."

-Darlene Schacht

Patrice Matthews

Contributing Author

Let's Werk !!!

"The only bad exercise is the one you skipped", Amit Kalantri, Wealth of Words. With this quote, wellness comes to mind. It's an active process of becoming aware and making choices towards a healthy and fulfilling life. Wellness is more than being free from illness; it is a dynamic process of change and growth. It is a state of complete physical, mental, and social wellbeing. It also makes you feel great and confident about yourself. A well-known actress once said, "if you prioritize yourself, you are going to save yourself," Gabrielle Union.'

While wellness has many different meanings, the one which resonates with me the most is the quality of being in good health, with an actively sought goal.

At the age of five-years-old, my mother enrolled me in dance classes. I participated in African dance, modern dance, and ballet. Whether I was in dance class, in the car or home listening to music. The music resonated within my body on how it would move towards the beat. Dancing made me feel as if I was the only person in the room. While dancing, I could express whatever I was feeling through music. When I was finished, whatever I felt before, immediately disappeared. Dancing was a form of therapy for me, making it impossible not to teach during this pandemic. At first, I pondered what I would do to keep fit and motivate my students to do the same. I asked myself, "What can I do to bring the same enthusiasm and energy virtually?" Immediately I took to social media to continue to connect to my students. There were several instructors already teaching classes virtually. I sent a survey through my social media page about how many students would be interested, if I continued using the Zoom format. The response was well-received, and at first, I offered classes free of charge. Once class size increased, I charged a fee that would be applicable even during this pandemic. Classes were amazing, continuing to have fitness classes at the same time as my in-person class schedule. Being able to see my students in the comforts of their own home was a joy to them and me. I started broadcasting my classes in my dining area- and later confirmed my basement to a studio with streamers and lights. After setting up my studio in my basement, I felt a sense of pride and accomplishment. Now mind you, this is something I've been meaning to do since we moved into the house 20 years ago. Like the woman in the insurance company commercial, I wanted my own, "She Shed."

As for the rest of my family, one hour a day, 3 days a week, they heard nothing but bass. On occasion, my 20-year-old daughter would make an appearance to show me how she thinks it should be done. Being on video was somewhat out of my comfort zone. I am used to teaching people and love feeling the energy of my students in person. But this helped me to build my confidence and decide to film more. I was determined to continue to offer my students class on the same schedule. Despite having several technical challenges, I had to learn how to make my playlist compatible with Zoom. In addition to the lighting, connectivity issues, and just conforming to this new world we are living in. This pandemic was out of my control; however, I would not allow it to defeat me and my goals. Working from home was very stressful for me, in addition to those taking my virtual classes. However, having my class schedule with Zoom helped me anticipate the class as relief from current working conditions. Several of my students have been a part of my journey as an instructor since I began teaching in 2011; they have become like family. I wanted to ensure they were getting the most from virtual classes as in person. I asked them what they liked about having class virtually, in addition to what they expected during this difficult time. They agreed! To see each other and embrace though music helped them forget about their workday. We all shared the same frustrations of not being able to physically be in the same space and dance together. We typically have dance battles in class, where one side competes against the other; this is difficult to do via live stream. Trust me, I'm trying to figure it out, though! While teaching, I get lost in the music. I enjoy seeing the excitement and determination on my students face along with the same enjoyment and passion. I felt their energy through the computer screen, which was more than enough for me.

One of the many things I love about Zumba is the annual conventions in July in Orlando, Florida. I have attended convention since 2013, this will be the first year that I missed. This is an opportunity for us to engage with instructors from around the world. Learning from the best of the best, being with Zumba's founder and those that teach through videos. It's like a big party for four days.

I look forward to this time; now, all I have are the memories of past conventions that appear on my social media feed.

Even with my Zumba classes that I teach, daily walks in my neighborhood park, I have managed to gain a few pounds eating cookies and some of my other favorite snacks. I had to get a grip on staying away from snacks and concentrate on healthier options. I started tracking my calories, limiting bread, carbs, and sugar to get back to where I was- before the pandemic. Food was a familiar way of comfort for the unknown, the unfamiliar, and it tastes good. But this too would not help my fitness goal-once this pandemic is over. Before Covid19, I handled my diet better- because there were places to go, such as shopping, visiting friends, and family, just getting out of the house. My house was my comfort zone, now it was my place of employment, gym, with no way of escape. I found myself wandering from the basement to the bedroom with no end in sight.

I had to reflect on a quote from Maya Angelou, "You are the sum of everything you've ever seen, heard, eaten, smelled, been told, forgot- it's all there. Everything influences each of us, and because of that, I try to make sure that my experiences are positive." This quote brought me back to the reality- that this, too, shall pass.

It may be a while before this pandemic is over. If we continue to follow the guidelines set, such as wearing a mask in public, washing our hands, and sanitizing our possessions. We can all come out of this current situation. For now, I will continue to offer my class via live stream on the Zoom format. I have participated with another Zumba instructor in an outdoor community class; social-distancing and masks were worn. This gave us positive insight that we can meet in public if these measures are taken into consideration. Quite a few of our students attended; they also thoroughly enjoyed the outdoor class. The consideration is in place to have the outdoor classes regularly. Of course, weather permitting. Additionally, following a healthier diet and reaching others will positively help to continue to motivate others. I have also added strength training to my schedule, which assists with full-body toning and not just dancing.

I would like to close by asking you to ask yourself, what will you do to keep your wellness? How will you ensure your success? Will you continue virtually? Are you opposed to live, outdoor classes? Will you ever go back to your local gym? These are questions many are asking themselves to maintain their health and wellness. This year has proven to be very Unprecedented times; with that said, I can rely on a quote from Sadie Tanner Mosely Alexander- "Don't let anything stop you. There will be times when you'll be disappointed, but you can't stop. Make yourself the best that you can make out of what you are. The very best."

RETINA M. CARTER

Contributing Author

Preserve My Peace

*"Peace I leave with you, my peace I give
unto you: not as the world giveth, give I
unto you. Let not your heart be troubled,
neither let it be afraid."*
The Bible: John 14:27 KJV

"Babe... Can you do your work in the garage?"

Yes, these are the exact words from my husband to me after day one of remote working and virtual learning for our four children. I laughed and halfway thought he was kidding around. After 16 years of marriage, the tiny micro-expressions on his face were quite familiar to me. My laughter stopped; and, I asked him why he would suggest such a thing. I added in a zinger that he was also a loud talker during phone calls.

Nonetheless, a wonderfully patient man, he went on to explain that while my headset allowed me to focus on *my* conversation, I was a loud talker and disturbing *his* work. I'd love to tell you that I accepted the feedback. We reached a resolution on the allocation of the workspace for maximum productivity; but, let's just say that did not happen...until cooler emotions prevailed, later...

This chapter is dedicated to the reality of what it means to have a spouse and children all in the same space for months.

I'll share my journey through the relationships between spouses, children, and self. This journey revealed truly incredible lessons that fundamentally changed our family.

How did the workspace situation turn out? Well, what ensued was five minutes of intense fellowship. By the conclusion, I realized that all six of us being in the home created a lot of stress. My husband owns his own business and works from home some days and other days at a collaborative business office. So, the house, well, that's his space during the hours we are all away. He walks freely about during conference calls, listens to Christian music while strategizing, and makes his way to the kitchen to snack on goodies between calls. Now, we were all here, in this unfamiliar situation, doing our best to adapt. Adding to this were concerns with how the business would fare during this uncertain time. All this created stress.

Seeing that we were fussing about something that could easily be managed, I asked him if he would take an afternoon walk with me. We ventured out into our neighborhood for the first time in almost 15 years. We walked the entire subdivision. During that time, I listened to my husband-- I mean, really listened to what was on his heart. We found the time so amazing that the next day, we set time to walk again. Several months into the quarantine situation, we have made this a part of our daily routine.

As for the working space, we agreed that the children would be split between upstairs and downstairs. I claimed a spot on the first floor with the agreement that I would relocate to the upstairs at the time of my eldest daughter's daily call on google meet. Further, we established noon to one o'clock as family lunchtime. I would prepare lunch for the whole family. The children gave feedback that they loved having lunch with mom and dad. Our youngest declared that she wanted to keep remote learning going for the rest of the school year. Her words became life as school remained virtual for the balance of the 3rd and 4th quarters.

We had a routine and relative peace. We managed not to overload the wi-fi too much.

BUT, then, the violence across America caused us to draw closer than ever. It was then that my husband and I had discussions with our children that we thought were reserved for history lessons from the civil unrest of the 1960s. Yet, it was 2020. How could this be happening?

> *"Peacemakers who sow in peace reap a*
> *harvest of righteousness."*
> *The Bible: James 3: 18 NIV*

The pandemic forced the country to slow down just long enough to realize that critical injustices were happening to African American citizens. No longer could people so easily justify the murders of black people. The 8-minute death of George Floyd was on film for the entire world to see. Our children, confused, scared, and looking to us for answers, asked question after question. The one that broke me, "why don't they like us?" Holding back tears of anger, we did our best to walk through the HIStory that was not being taught in their classes. I spent time with my eldest daughter discussing books written by Booker T. Washington, W.E.B. Dubois, and several other black scholars. I made sure I heard each one of their concerns and addressed them. I began to take individual walks with each child and have found ways to spend regular time with each one individually.

We made sure to clarify that not all people were racists, but we needed them to know that a culture of systemic racism exists in this country. We reassured them that their beautiful brown skin was a special gift from God above. We showed our kids how our people responded to racism with strategic action. We let them see us as we participated in the Cincinnati marches, and learn about one of my special friend's who was instrumental in the organization of the "Black Lives Matter" mural located in downtown Cincinnati. Our family began to actively support more black-owned businesses. We needed to have our children see that black-owned businesses operate with excellence and create value for the community far beyond the product or service rendered. Crucially, the books we curated for our children showed the beauty, intelligence, and tenacity of black people.

Teaching them about their history created vivid questions, and moments of laughter, and even somberness. After delving into our history, somehow, a sense of peace filled our home as the children began to speak about their ideas concerning our ancestors' accomplishments. Being present in the moment allowed me to take in this precious time and appreciate it. Yet, as the days turned into weeks, it became more challenging to balance the family's needs with work and self-care.

*"Be careful for nothing; but in everything
by prayer and supplication with
thanksgiving let your requests be made
known unto God."
The Bible: Phil. 4:6 KJV*

After one week where the workday extended well into the evening hours, it became clear that something needed to change in the work-life balance. Clothes were fitting a little more snugly, and although noon to one was designated lunch time, meetings kept creeping in and taking over.

One morning after devotional, it came to me that time needed to be recaptured in the schedule. This started with adding focus time at 8am, 12pm, and 4pm into the calendar. This created the time to exercise or process through emails. This helped me to reduce the number of early morning or late afternoon meetings. Online workouts became a part of the routine as well. With a friend, I added in some accountability using my Apple watch. Both acts as accountability partners for my activity, and they keep me honest with staying up on movement calories, standing time, and exercise time.

Around this time, a friend shared a shout on social media about her meal prep business. We couldn't pass up the ease of having healthy, tasty meals prepared at a reasonable cost, making lunchtime far more exciting than ever. Also, since the kids were out of school and in camp, there were only two of us in the house. It was the best thing for us! Even after we return to work in the office, part of our weekly budget will include pre-

prepared meals. I knew that I needed balance. It came with prepared meals, fitness accountability, and use of focus time to make room for exercise and productivity.

Final Thoughts & Call to Action

This unprecedented time gave occasion to listen more, communicate better, and take care of self and family's needs in a different way. It has been a blessing to spend every evening walking a couple of miles with my husband. Not only did we get time to de-stress from the workday, but we also used this time to keep our bond together. Our children are wiser and more educated about the world and black history. Further, we believe they are proud to be of African ancestry. My fitness journey continues to go strongly thanks to the flexibility of adjusting to online workouts and the incorporation of meal planning. I am thankful for the blessing of being in this time and season of life. I want you to think through how you can enhance your family communications, take care of yourself, and enrich your relationships. Use this time to make an imprint that will leave a lasting impact. Love, peace, and joy. ~ RMC.

DIANNA L. PLEASANT

Contributing Author

Faith It Til YOU Make It:
Sustaining Your Seed of Faith During This Unprecedented Time

Planting the Seed

"Faith is taking the first step, even when you don't see the full staircase."
– Martin Luther King, Jr.

Sitting on the window ledge of my living room, I can see the dark clouds getting ready to generate mayhem outside. These brewing storm clouds outside of my home remind me of the current storms facing my life. I find myself in a waiting season that is bringing with it plenty of impending changes. All these recent changes in my life have stirred up some anxiety in my soul; why am I once again single after a longstanding relationship that I was sure would one day lead me walking down the aisle? Will I ever get married or have children? How will I keep myself and students safe this upcoming school year with the increase of COVID-19 cases? And will I ever be able to walk and bend my leg normal again with no pain; after recently recovering from not one, but two surgeries on my left leg from a serious ATV accident the previous year?

As I sought God about my current anxieties and the uncertainties about my future, I couldn't help but wonder if I was experiencing this emotional and spiritual distress because I was being punished for something I had done that displeased God. But the Lord spoke to me and said, "When you were younger, I already prepared and planted the seed of faith in you for the changes that are coming, all you have to do is water it. These current circumstances in your life force you to exercise your faith in me more now than ever. Be not dismayed, for I am with you during these unprecedented times. All you have to do is just trust and believe in me; the one and only true living God."

Promoting the Growth

> "To one who has faith, no explanation is necessary. To one without faith, no explanation is possible."

— Italian Philosopher, Thomas Aquinas

One of my best girlfriends, knowing about my current struggles, said, "You always have a smile on your face!" Others have said, "I don't know how you can stay so positive with all that's going on in the world right now!" Unfortunately, I don't have any supernatural power to hold it together or endure these testing times. I have learned that the recipe to having faith in God, even during the most devastating storms, isn't effortless or easy. This type of faith takes time and commitment. You can't always wait until the most problematic things in your life happen to apply and practice faith. It's favorable to exercise one's faith when things are going good too.

The Bible goes into great detail about having faith in God's love and sovereignty. I mentioned the brewing storm clouds outside my living room window, but I was safe, warm, and dry inside my home. This is the same safety that our Lord and Savior offers us, even amidst the storms of life. "God is our refuge and strength, an ever-present help in trouble." (Psalm 46:1 NIV). To have faith in God during these challenging and unprecedented times, we have to be rooted in Him. We have to know our Heavenly Father before we will trust Him and His plans.

Producing the Harvest

*"Feed your faith and your fears will starve
to death."*

Many people don't believe in things that they cannot see. They focus on a number of disappointing causes and effects, failing to identify the small miracles in life that time after time work in our favor. There's an enormous level of responsibility for having faith in life. People have moved mountains with their faith. Even when situations seemed dire and bleak, it was their faith that carried them through. "And Jesus answered them, "Have faith in God. Truly, I say to you, whoever says to this mountain, 'Be taken up and thrown into the sea,' and does not doubt in his heart, but believes that what he says will come to pass, it will be done for him. Therefore I tell you, whatever you ask in prayer, believe that you have received it, and it will be yours." (Mark 11:22-24)

As a Believer of Christ, you have to know that faith is just as important as the air we breathe. While the oxygen in the air nourishes the body, faith nourishes the mind, heart, and soul. It's the energy that should be trickling through every single fiber and cell within our beings. Faith should be a part of every muscle and every strand of thought. It is the fundamental foundation of our existence. While life can be hard at the worst of times, faith knows deep down inside that things will get better. "Now faith is the substance of things hoped for, the evidence of things not seen." (Hebrews 11:1 KJV) Having faith in what is to come, and losing our fears in self-giving love and service for Christ will lead to a happier and more fulfilling life. Faith shouldn't be just a belief that Christians hold onto during tested times; faith is a much-needed element to all human life.

So how can YOU sustain your seed of faith during this unprecedented time?

"Unprecedented times call for unprecedented faith!"

Action Steps:

1. ***YOU must have a heart of forgiveness***. If you think you can receive a miracle with bitterness in your heart? Think again. You have to go before the Lord and ask Him to reveal to you anyone you haven't forgiven in your life (this could go way back). Write down everyone who comes to mind and ask God to help you forgive those individuals who have hurt or disappointed you at some time in your life.

2. ***YOU must refuse to entertain doubt-filled thoughts***. You must focus on positivity and train

your mind to think in abundance. In times of trouble, we tend to move away from positivity. We go from a state of abundance to a state of lack. But, faith is the tool that helps replenish abundance in the heart and the spirit, not just in the mind. Whatever it is that we focus on in life, we get more of. If we focus on problems, we live solely in those problems and have difficulty moving past the negativity. You must focus on positivity and seek out solutions to resolve your problems and move from a state of lack back to a state of abundance.

3. ***YOU have to sharpen your listening skills***. God wants you to receive your miracle, and He has some special instructions for you. Can you hear Him if you're wrapped up in thinking about your troubles or needs? The noise in your head can be loud enough to block out God's still, small voice. Be intentional about getting quiet before the Lord and identifying and listening to His voice. When you hear from the Lord, He will give you the instructions that will lead you to receive your miracle.

4. ***YOU need to speak the language of faith and do something***. *"Faith without works is dead."* (James *2:26 NKJV)* As important as it is to resist doubt, faith alone won't get the whole job done. You can't just sit around believing on the inside and do nothing on the outside. For faith to come alive, you have to take action. If you need something to

harvest, have you planted anything? To reap a spiritual harvest, you've got to plant the Word of God in your heart. When you believe in your heart and say with your mouth what you want from God, that is when you can receive it.

5. **YOU have to 100% yield to God and His perfect will.** "Trust in the Lord with all thine heart, and lean not unto thine own understanding. In all thy ways acknowledge him, and he shall direct thy paths." (Proverbs 3:5-6 KJV) God can heal the hurt, fix the broken, and give strength to the weak. He rescued a messed up sinner like me and continues to mold me into something beautiful. He did it for me, and He will do it for you if just believe and have faith. Step into the fullness of what God has planned for your life. You must be willing to leave your comfort zone and pursue the way that God's Spirit leads. Not thine will, but Your will, Heavenly Father.

6. **YOU have to learn the art of waiting and expect the impossible.** Often, the difference between receiving a miracle and not receiving comes down to your willingness to wait. Patience keeps your faith strong until you cross the finish line. You have to develop the kind of patience that knows if you believe it, you will receive it. Having patience and a spirit of expectancy holds the door of faith open and is a key to receiving your miracle. If you only see the natural realm of possibilities - that's not faith!

Kirsten L. Van Kallen Hampton

Contributing Author

7. Happiness is Earned Not Given

Happiness is what we all want out of life, right? Unfortunately, like most great things in life, being happy takes work. Why? You may ask. Because happiness is something that only you can give yourself. An American writer once said, "Happiness doesn't depend on any external conditions, it is governed by our mental attitude." Therefore, one cannot look for happiness in someone or something because, at any moment, those things can be gone, and you will be left yearning to fill the void. COVID 19 came and smacked us all in the face. What many of us thought would be a quick couple of weeks off of work turned into months of isolation, worry, and so much more. Most, if not all, of the things that make us happy, was quickly taken away, and we were left to cope with what has become our new reality.

For me, one of the primary things that have been taken away has been my ability to travel. Traveling has been something I've been doing almost my whole entire life. One of my earliest memories of traveling and probably my first international trip was at three years old to visit my family in Holland. I remember visiting the Heineken factory and drinking the alcohol-free beer for children, buying a Dutch sausage called bloedworst from street vendors, and meeting and playing with my older cousins for the first time. My parents instilled an affinity for traveling within me that remains within me to this day. Today, it is one of my most favorite things to do and my biggest stress reliever. I keep a trip on my calendar at all times. When I am having a hard day at work, I think about my upcoming trip, and my attitude is quickly adjusted. When I am overwhelmed with everything I have on my plate, I think about the next trip, and the load feels a tad bit lighter.

Don't trip when you can't take a trip

In the midst of this worldwide pandemic, traveling, my most favorite thing to do, is one of the most cautioned activities for immune-compromised individuals, like myself. In March 2020, when the world essentially shut down, I had two trips planned. St. Thomas in June and Curacao in July. While the pandemic was devastating and inconvenient for many, I was looking forward to staying home, relaxing, and getting a much-needed break from work and, simply put, life. However, by month two of our countrywide shutdown, when my much-needed break began to turn to boredom, I thought about my upcoming trips, and I was able to maintain my sanity. At the beginning of June, our first trip was canceled, and shortly after, so was the second trip. I literally felt myself spiraling thinking about being stuck in Cincinnati with nowhere to go and no idea of when I'd be able to travel again. Not only is traveling one of my favorite things to do, but it provides me with the ability to visit my family often, as my husband nor I have any biological family in Cincinnati or close driving distance. Therefore, traveling was taken away from me, but so was my next favorite thing, my family.

As I previously mentioned, I began to spiral from the seemingly happy-go-lucky me to a sad and anxious person I didn't recognize. The foreseeable future included me in Cincinnati with little to no information regarding when it would be safe for the vulnerable population to travel. I had nothing to look forward to, or distract me from the difficult reality. As my eagerness to travel began to grow, despite our country's condition, this inability to travel became a point of contention in my household. I was forced to sit down and evaluate the whole situation and how I would deal with my inability to fulfill my desire. After much thought, I realized that I had been using traveling, for most of my adult life, to escape life's challenges. In this particular instance, traveling was used as a means to escape a city that I don't love. Instead of creating my happiness in Cincinnati, I sought refuge everywhere else. While I make it a known fact, to everyone I meet, that I am and will always be an L.A. girl, Cincinnati is now my home. Traveling could no longer be an escape to find happiness because, at this time, it just simply wasn't an option. I'd have to resolve my issues and find happiness within me. You have to make a conscious decision to choose happiness every day, despite what is thrown your way. When life hands you lemons, all you can do is make lemonade, and that is where the work comes in.

Put In the Work!

Like marriage, running a business, and anything else rewarding, being happy takes work. The first step is mentally committing to letting go of anxiety, sadness, complaining, and any other negativity that impedes your happiness. Now, that doesn't mean that all your problems will disappear after doing so, but committing to letting go of negativity is the first step in working towards your happiness. Direct your focus to things you have been blessed with, instead of the things that create challenges for you in your life. Regardless of what issues you may have, you can always find something you have been blessed with, even if it is waking up in the morning with your functioning five senses. I have a loving husband, a beautiful home, family in good health, a bunch of great friends right here in Cincinnati, and so much more. This first task alone helped tremendously in my journey to finding peace and happiness within.

Next, seek out things you enjoy doing. Think about something you loved to do as a child that you stopped doing. Think about things you used to enjoy but no longer have time to do or simply forgot about. A few of those things for me were crocheting, reading, horseback riding, sketching, and creating random things like bookmarks that I could sell for fifty cents (I thought I was rich back in the day). Instead of spending each day of quarantine trying to determine the cost-benefit analysis of taking a flight to California, I began working on different activities I enjoy daily. As I crocheted scarves, sketched, and even worked out, I began to think less and less about my grievances. Once you embrace your situation and start doing things you genuinely enjoy, you can find joy and peace. Engaging in activities you enjoy creates a positive atmosphere and makes space for happiness in your life.

The most crucial step to finding happiness within is reprogramming your brain to be happy. It sounds like this would be an easy task, and for some, it might be. However, it takes time and constant reminders to get to that place. I must say I haven't mastered this yet, but I am actively working on it. Prayer, meditation, and reciting affirmations are a few tools you can use to help you find and maintain happiness. When I moved to Cincinnati, I intended to leave as soon as the appropriate time came. But when my circumstances changed, my mindset didn't, and that is why I made it a point to book a trip out of town as often as possible. It wasn't until I reprogrammed my brain that I could fully embrace the city I live in as my home and find happiness with the cards that I have been dealt with. Like committing to letting go of negativity, you must commit to being happy. When you feel yourself falling short of your commitment, that is the perfect time to use your tools to re-center yourself.

The power of our thoughts and ideas are forces that are unknown and underestimated by many. Our thoughts and ideas play factors in our failures, successes, sadness, and happiness. Happiness is a decision that only we can control through our thoughts and ideas. You can let adversity bring you down, or you can find the lesson or blessing in the challenges you face and choose happiness. External factors are nothing more than things that help build our character, not determinants of our fate. It took a world pandemic for me to sit down and take control of my happiness. What will it take for you to take control of yours?

Danielle Battle

Contributing Author

Trailblazing the Path of Leadership

Life moments are always defined by learning experiences that build character. Organic learning experiences can cultivate foundational leadership skills. These leadership skills are often tested throughout one's life, giving credence to one's morals and values. They provide a path for an individual to navigate their way through life. Learning how to be a change agent for yourself, family, and community.

Who would have known that the ideals of servant leadership started for a young girl, in the corner of a kitchen, with a simple tea set? This young girl embraced her mother's stories and teachings while always making sure that her mothers' teacup was full. From the same kitchen area, she watched her mother prepare the many meals that fostered more conversations about life and education. The young girl may not have fully understood at the time that she was developing her skills of giving back to her community, being family-oriented, and the importance of education. She started that process by learning to listen to others and making them feel valued. She emulated servant leadership by demonstrating her willingness to place others above herself as she learned how to navigate life. As her servant leadership style continued to develop, she began to embrace a transformational leader elements. This shift in serving others evolved into working with and for those without voice, experiencing inequities and inequality.

Transformational leadership invites others' participation in all processes that aim to attain organizational goals. An essential aspect of such a process is learning. Learning for a leader implies that the leader is open to listening to others, reflects on what needs to be done, and accepts that he/she does not have all of the answers or solutions to perform the work at hand. What unfolds is a leader's enactment of a process of learning that recognizes the importance of engagement for solving complex problems. In times of crisis, a leader needs to be adaptable, courageous, risk-taking, and willing to allow others to participate in a manner that demonstrates shared responsibilities in the shaping and attaining individual and shared goals within the community.

How does transformational leadership play a role in school administration?

School administration is a fluid position because it can be described and understood through the scope of various theories, studies, and adopted measures. It is transformational. An effective leader rises to the occasion, continuously shaping the vision fueled by identifying a necessary change for creating and sustaining success. The ability to recognize when change is needed is a vital skill of a school leader. How has your 'why' empowered you through your leadership journey?

As a school leader, he/she must have the innate ability to be visionary and cutting edge in unprecedented times. It also requires the leader to identify the inequities and opportunities for the constituents they serve.

The school leader needs to fight hard to shape student success conditions by building relationships with all of the stakeholders in the community. They also need to promote opportunities for all stakeholders to contribute to the school's success and create conditions that fostered growth and learning for all. Ultimately the administrator needs to believe student academic success required fulfillment of the school's mission and vision of developing the 'whole student.' Emphasis on the 'whole student' will allow the school to create rigorous and realistic programming, providing the necessary academic, social, and emotional support. The 'whole student' educational journey can be defined with learning experiences relevant to the students' needs and educational goals. Support for those initiatives is often facilitated through community outreach opportunities. Many community partners give the school the tools and resources needed to provide a nurturing environment to all students. This drive to connect all stakeholders within a community will expand the transformational lens to a focus on educational leadership, public education, community engagement, and politics.

The young trailblazer previously mentioned was able to extend her reach in the community and develop and implement initiatives that focused on student academic success. She used these platforms to ensure all learning opportunities were equitable and accessible, and students were provided the conditions and tools necessary for achievement. As she continued to pave her way through the world of education, she actualized her dream to become a doctor, she finally earned her Ph.D. in

Educational Leadership. Currently, serving on several executive boards, she can create and implement initiatives that focus on helping young people become self-sufficient adults in their community. She shares her expertise and provides input and guidance for the successful implementation of innovative educational programs. She takes time to recognize the natural interdependence that exists among the people in a community. Ultimately, being the change agent, the community needs to ensure everyone has an opportunity to contribute to help their community thrive and attain its goals. She made it her life ministry to share this knowledge to improve schools and their communities' viability—a true trailblazer in the world of education.

Reflecting on your leadership journey, remember a leader not only performs through a lens of best practices, but also through innate abilities that are closely associated with creativity, innovation, and discovery. The leader knows that each situation lends itself to specific elements of a servant and transformational leadership skills. As a servant leader, one is competent in fulfilling his/her responsibilities and caring and places service above self. As a transformational leader, one is not only courageous but also humble because he/she does not act with others from a position of authority but operates with others from a place of shared values and responsibilities. How can you use the skills of a servant and transformational leader to empower yourself and others?

TAMMY L. SOLOMON-GRAY

Contributing Author

Calling All Revolutionary Parents and Educators

Revolutionary, as defined by Merriam-Webster, is, "activity or movement designed to effect fundamental changes in the socioeconomic situation; a fundamental change in the way of thinking about or visualizing something: a change of paradigm" Whether you are a parent or an educator, the idea that somehow your calling, your role, your life's work can be, should be and is revolutionary may sound huge. However, the work itself, while important, is simple. The harvest of the outcomes for our children is monumental. There is a tremendous number of revolutionary parents and teachers living among us. You may already be a revolutionary, or you may be striving to become a revolutionary. With consistent attention to your child's or student's growth, humility to seek wise counsel, and willingness to understand all team members that help you in the educational setting, you, too, can be a revolutionary!

As a veteran Elementary Principal, I have developed an intimate and extensive recognition of the many ways that parental agreements are absent to be peaceable toward one another. Simultaneously, co-parenting or respectful in moments of disagreement with members of the school village harms children. The absence of mutual respect handicaps the social and educational growth of innocent children. Meanwhile, children whose parents have made the small yet critical decision to model respectful exchanges at home and at the schoolhouse thrive and grow into individuals who are beyond prepared to excel at each level and grade. It is past time for a parental and educator revolution of systemic proportions. That being said, there are everyday revolutionary parents and educators on the front lines, shifting paradigms, making a few but powerful choices on behalf of children. The choices are shared with "the village," which guarantees positive outcomes for their children and students.

The first revolutionary that I ever met read to me every night, after working full-time and a part-time job, by the light of my Winnie the Pooh lamp. My mother had to be beyond exhausted! I know this because my son is 27 years old, and for the lion-share of his childhood, I was teaching and going to school full time, and I know that I was dead-dog tired, but the revolutionary presses on. Ensuring that her daughter was read to every night was an act of revolution because it was an act of sacrifice and seed-planting. No one, including myself, would judge a hard-working parent to feed their children, give them their bath, and put them to bed as anything but a good parent. The revolutionary parent, however, looks forward to the future and reflects on the following question, "What can I do now to ensure that my child ends up in a better place than the one that I'm in when they become my age?" Having that space and time at the end of the day exploring new books or rereading a favorite book for the hundredth time meant everything to me, and it made me want to read independently, just like my mama.

Early childhood development (birth to 5 years old) is tremendous growth and developmental period. In fact, there is no other five year period in life that has as much growth and potential than early childhood. The revolution must begin with conversations and observations between the adults who care for the children, parents, extended family, and friends, also known as "the village." Every school year, in grades, Pre-Kindergarten through First Grade (Preschool is the new Kindergarten; write that down and tell every parent of a toddler in your Village), I am astounded by my youngest's growth. Students from August to January!

Kindergarteners go from singing ABCs to learning that letters make sounds and sounds make words and words make sentences, then ta-dah, in January, five-year-olds are making simple sentences and reading beginner books. First graders are writing simple research projects and presenting them to their teachers and classmates. It's truly a beautiful thing to watch!

Sometimes, this is not the image and growth that a revolutionary parent sees. The cloudy vision can be anything from the child being reluctant to connect with the teacher to have greater needs than previously known. The revolutionary parent uses Stephen Covey's Habit 5, "Seek First to Understand, Then to be Understood," to avoid jumping to under-informed conclusions. Questioning the caretakers, educators, and other Village members with more experience with school-age children is a continuous action that should not stop until graduation from high school. Questioning is the path to answers and problem-solving. But what happens when there is a quiver in the stomach that something is just not right with your child's school? What does a revolutionary parent do when it becomes crystal clear that their child is not being challenged in their school environment?

My mother found herself in that very predicament during my kindergarten year. In speaking with her "Village," she learned that there were "Magnet/Alternative Schools" with specialized instructional programs to enroll me. The revolutionary parent does not waste time on things beyond their control but instead focuses on their available levers of control. Revolutionary parents recognize that their time and energy are best spent focused on the important things to their children's development and growth. Sometimes that's easier said than done. Revolutionary parents have to figure out which human levers in their Village to activate to support them in making the crooked paths straight for their children to have a solid educational foundation.

The revolutionary parent also knows their children, inside and out. When we revolutionary educators have to call home to speak with one of our revolutionary parents, begin with a respectful greeting and tone. Parents, it is a spiritual trap to be offended by being asked to support the Village, at school, or anywhere else with your child's imperfections. By all means, be annoyed, be frustrated, and be concerned but do not be confused; the Village at the schoolhouse is a kind and joyful partner with parents and guardians, not an adversary against them or their children.

As a revolutionary parent leads their child and collaborates with the Schoolhouse Village, there may be times when constructive conflict becomes necessary. I define constructive conflict as "Conflict that emerges after a review and reflection of services or performance is not mutually acceptable to both parties. While respectful in nature, there is a push and pull that results in an alternative outcome."

Over the years as a classroom teacher and now as a principal, I have experienced multiple instances of constructive conflict. These conflicts can stretch and grow both the revolutionary parent and educator. The greatest of my conflicts occurred when I was a third-grade teacher on a Special Education team for one of my students. Revolutionary educators are open to constructive conflict and provide revolutionary parents the space to express their concerns and THEN work towards a new option that is mutually acceptable. One of the child's parents worked at a social service agency, and they shared with us how they were asked, every day, by some clients to read or explain very basic information that they should have been able to process independently. The parents did not want their daughter to be vulnerable in society, and the learning goals that we initially wrote for her would, in their opinion, leave her in a vulnerable space as an adult.

There was a time, not so long ago, when parent involvement looked like Room Mothers, cupcakes, and carpools. While these images are good, parent involvement in the 21st century is largely about communication and positive relationships between parents and school staff. The newer modes of communication may be emails, text messages, virtual meetings, and conferences. There is no shame in utilizing these methods, at times, that best fits your busy schedule. For best results, choose 2-3 times, which will give you and your child's school team mutually convenient opportunities for maximizing your child's success.

Cara Owsley

Contributing Author

Isolation
Girl Are You Experiencing Loneliness?
You are not alone

"People who are alone, are often not lonely,
and people who are lonely, are often not
alone, which one are you?" ~ unknown

I've experienced some tough times in my life, including an abusive husband that I divorced after only being married for two years. A couple of years later, my 5-year-old daughter and I were displaced after losing our home to the floodwaters of Hurricane Katrina. But even in the midst of those challenging chapters in my life, I never felt alone or lonely. I was always surrounded by people; family and friends, who encouraged and supported with words and acts of kindness. They would take us out to dinner, to the movie theater and even shopping.

The Change in Times Changed my Emotions

This recent test, brought on by the Coronavirus pandemic, proved to be something entirely different. I experienced an emotion I had never felt in 48 years of life. This feeling was something I couldn't describe. I kept telling myself, "Girl, you have been through a lot of stuff, you will get over it." "Girl, you escaped a horrible marriage with a 2-year-old daughter.' "Girl, you moved and got your dream job as a staff photojournalist at The Times-Picayune." "Girl, you survived being homeless because of a hurricane." After this talk with myself, I finally said, "Surely, girl, if I can get through all of that, you can get through this."

But I had never lived during a pandemic. Nor had I worked from home for months at a time. The world that we knew dramatically changed. I have never been cut off from seeing my family and friends or seeing my girlfriends two to three times a week at Zumba class; happy hours after work with friends were gone, too. The virus changed everything. For several weeks, I couldn't shake — or even identify — what I was feeling inside, all I knew is "this" feeling was different.

Finally, I realized I was lonely, and the isolation hit me hard. A few weeks into the stay-at-home order, I had already been off work, recovering from a hysterectomy, so my contact with people was already limited, Netflix and judge shows on television only go so far. I have been a photojournalist for 25 years. I love interacting every day with people. I love smiling and laughing. I love hearing about their lives and work. Working from home and limiting what assignments my Cincinnati Enquirer visuals staff would cover because the Coronavirus left an empty space in me and left me without my normal energy. Even when I did get outside to work, the majority of people's smiles are covered with a mask. Working from home was also very stressful. I was not efficient. I felt as though I worked longer hours and seemed to be on more Zoom meetings than we had in person when working in the office. I often felt like I could never take a break at my own home. I was afraid I would miss an email, a text message, phone call or an instant message from a colleague. The constant dings from the notifications became overwhelming at times and piqued my anxiety.

I knew I had to battle these negative feelings. But how?

How to improve your mental health?

Pray and asked God to help you. Read scriptures for comfort and peace. Develop an intentional but achievable plan to beat the loneliness. Consider some tidbits that worked for me:

First, figure out how to manage your day better during the "workday."

Second, be more proactive with your relationships with family and friends.

Third, GET OUT OF THE HOUSE! Don't do like me just going to the grocery to get some healthy items, but also getting my favorites M&M's and wine, not necessary consumed at the same time. Also, take the time to feel the sun on your skin, to smell the fresh air, and to burn some calories. The quarantine 15 (pounds) was real for me.

Plan to conquer loneliness:

Start your day with giving thanks and talking with God about whatever was on your mind and reading a devotional.

Second, I learned that I needed to reach out more to my family and friends.

Third, consistent exercise was necessary, as much for my mental health as my physical health.

For my daily reading I use the You Version Bible App; it's loaded with a wide range of study plans. I don't let my day get started without this, even if I am in a rush and only have five minutes. My morning devotional is a priority and helps set the tone for my day. One of the most profound things I came away with from reading several different devotionals, "It's okay to be afraid or feel lonely at times, but we don't have to sit in that fear or loneliness." I memorized Psalm 91: 9-11 and would recite it to myself when I felt afraid or lonely.

Verse 9: If you make the Lord your refuge, if you make the Most High your shelter,

10: no evil will conquer you; no plague will come near your home. 11: For he will order his angels to protect you wherever you go.

In my pursuit to stay connected with family and friends, I subscribed to a Zoom account to allow me to talk with several of my girlfriends at one time. I have hosted "Zoom happy hours." We now look forward to just chat calls or specific prayer calls. I also have enjoyed several social distance lunches or dinner meet-ups. I also started sending greeting cards to family and friends. If I am experiencing loneliness, maybe others have, too.

The last key element to overcome the loneliness is exercise. Exercise is part of my self-care regiment. Daily walks in my neighborhood or the park has become my therapy. Listening to music while I walk and seeing the sun make me feel fresh and renewed. I love looking at the sky. Reflections on the lake make me sense all of God's creation. I smile at memories of going out on the water in the pedal boats with my daughter. These outings break-up my day while working from home; my house no longer feels like a prison. I am happier there now. As a manager at work, I felt drained by the several virtual meetings every day; could I ever unplug myself from my laptop? One day I had seven meetings! Can you relate to a sister? It's exhausting. Finally, I learned that I could leave my laptop. Most days I do a 30-minute workout early after my devotional and coffee. Later, I find time in between meetings to go for a walk in my neighborhood. Make sure you make time to get to take a break and do something for yourself.

My plans to conquer loneliness have made a huge positive difference for me, I don't have those consistent emotions of not feeling like "my always joyful self." I am grateful that I learned that I have to set boundaries to not become overwhelmed when it comes to working. I learned that I could set limits while working at home, just as I had established limits as a manager when we were in the office. I am grateful that I learned more about myself. And I hope that you can learn from your challenges as well. I am sure as the pandemic continues and other trials come, we will continue to learn more and will see this as a challenge to grow.

1.   I go often to this passage from James 1:2-8 (NLT):

2. Dear brothers and sisters, when troubles of any kind come your way, consider it an opportunity for great joy.

3. For you know that when your faith is tested, your endurance has a chance to grow. 4 So let it grow, for when your endurance is fully developed, you will be perfect and complete, needing nothing.

I feel more like myself now. And this is what I'm hearing from my inner voice: "Girl, you and God got this. You know you get in trouble when you think you can do it alone. God didn't bring you this far to leave you here now."

Carrita A. Hightower, PhD

Contributing Author

#Phenomenal Faith

"When you are in trouble and worried and sick at heart And your plans are upset and your world falls apart, Remember God's ready and waiting to share The burden you find much too heavy to bear– So with faith, "Let Go and Let GOD" lead your way."
Helen Steiner Rice

(Acapella humming and hands clapping)- "We come this far by faith...oh...leaning on the Lord..." My family is swaying in the warmth of our voices singing the family hymn. A song belted out at every family gathering- reminding us of our life's journey. I look around and notice everyone smiling, relishing in the joy of being in the presence of one another, and giving honor to our creator for his grace and mercy. "Ring...ring"- the sound of a telephone disrupts the harmony of the sopranos and altos. I think who has the nerve to have their phone on during the family's anthem. "Ring...ring"- the sound is even louder than before.

I shudder and awake from my Sunday afternoon slumber. It's my telephone ringing. I answer with a rasp in my voice, "H-e-l-l-o." My brother, in a calm yet shaken voice, says, "It's momma. She's been rushed to the emergency room. It's a stroke. She was at the afternoon church program." I am speechless, breathless, and instantly blind to the world around me.

In a flash, I am 13 years back in my dorm room, junior year of college. It is a Sunday afternoon. My mom has called- shaken, speaking slow and steady as possible- "It's your dad- he's gone. A massive heart attack." I freeze, speechless and blind.

"Rita...you there?" my brother yells with worry. I answer, "Yes- I am here. I am getting up and will be on my way to Memphis tonight."

This was eight years ago. I had no idea if my old yet reliable car would make the 500-mile drive from Ohio to Tennessee. I had only just started my career just two years prior and unsure how family medical leave worked. I had no clue how I would care for my mother, who would be paralyzed from an apricot sized brain bleed and assigned to a wheelchair for the rest of her life. I had no idea how I would afford the 24-hour in-home healthcare.

However, let me tell you what I knew to be true and believed with every fiber of my being; I knew I loved my mother, who lived a life of unshakable faith. I knew I was part of a family deeply rooted in resilient faith. The faith that brought us "this far" and would continue to carry us with "no turning back."

I took a leap of faith traveling 1-2 times per month, 1,000 miles round trip. I closely monitored her care, hired caregivers, drove her to physical/occupational therapy sessions. I leaned on my sister-cousin and brother to navigate her transfers from the hospital to assisted living to her own apartment in a senior living community chock full of amenities- making sure she had the best; she desired it.

I ***committed*** to this new way of life for my mom and our family. This included living between two states for over four years and watching a once fiercely independent woman accept the reality she would never live again in her home of 30+ years, never walk again, and only have the memories of a life she once knew. I modeled my mom's approach to this new way of life and committed to the idea "it is well with my soul."

I ***surrendered*** to the will of God. I was comforted knowing I had the strength of my family, my parents' teachings, and blind faith that has cradled us through the darkest of times.

I stepped back and watched God ***commence*** the work of grace and mercy in our lives. He is ready and waiting to help carry the load of life's trials and tribulations.

Are you ready to live a life of Phenomenal Faith? Add the formula and/or Playlist to your spiritual armor? Walk through times where faith is the size of a mustard seed, and more is needed?

Yes? Then, I welcome you to this journey of passionately pursuing Phenomenal Faith. As a scientist and aspiring Disc Jockey (Dr. DJ), I created a faith formula, playlist, and daily practices to (em)power you through unprecedented times.

Let the journey begin...

The Faith Formula:

Commitment + Surrendering + Watching God Commence = Phenomenal Faith

I realized each of these components was essential to honoring my mother and God's test of my trust and faith in his word.

The Challenge: Give this formula a try or create one of your own. Ask yourself, what am I doing to fuel my phenomenal faith? How have I committed, surrendered, and waited on God?

The Faith Playlist (authors/suggested performers):

I call this "Faith" hype music. When life seems daunting, one more phone call of despair, think/listen to lyrics of meaningful songs to fuel your faith. Let the words nurture your seeds of faith and transform your life. Here's my playlist...what will be yours?

1. "We've come this far by faith"- by Albert Goodson;

2. "It is well with my soul"- written by Horation Spafford; performed by Jennifer Holliday

3. "Lord do it for me right now"- written/performed by James Cleveland

4. "Hold on (Change is comin')"- performed by Sounds of Blackness

5. "Let Go"- performed by DeWayne Woods

6. "Your Spirit"- performed by Tasha Cobbs

The Challenge: Select a song to remind you of your faith walk and power to endure. Play it in your car, through your earbuds, or only in your mind.

Daily Practices:

Building any skill or changing a mindset requires time and practice. How will you develop your Faith muscle? Here are a few tips to get you started.

- Develop a Phenomenal Faith Mindset

- Create a purpose-driven Faith Statement (1-3 sentences); write it down on an index card, notes in your phone, a journal, a mirror...wherever you can see it daily

- Read it, memorize it. Let it remind you that your faith is the center of your purpose and strength.

- Practice a Faith Walk

- Gather your tribe (everyone has one). Enlist others to walk with you in the roles of guidance and/or support as you build, strengthen your faith.

- Take a walk- spend 10, 20, 30 minutes, walking and reflecting, releasing, and renewing yourself as well as your faith.

- Meditate- Create time and space to truly focus on your faith. Take a breath, close your eyes, and be still. This will bring clarity beyond belief. Trust me.

- Set Faith Goals

- Identify 3-5 faith goals
- Make them actionable, set a timeframe to reach your goals
- Celebrate regularly on achieving these goals
- Set new ones

I challenge you, if you remember nothing else from this reading, Unprecedented Times require Phenomenal Faith.

Love, Peace, and Faith be unto you, Dr. DJ

Kamyia Fletcher

Contributing Author

Amid a Pandemic...Their Education Matters

"Remember," he says as he holds the electric thermometer to my head, "You really only have two hours to get everything out."

"What happens if I'm not done by then?" I question as a chuckle and readjust my mask, so it is now covering my nose.

"I don't think we've gotten that far..." he quickly finished recording my "safe" temperature and badged me into the building. I thank him but can't help but think to myself the words he said. "We haven't gotten that far." I walk down the once colorful and noisy hallways previously filled with everything from sticky kindergarten to the AXE body spray of 6th graders, making their way to lunch. This hallway was not that. This hallway was dark. Stripped of all the colorful elementary banners. Student display work that once made me smile was now leftover staples and brick.

The colorful and encouraging posters. Gone.

The smell of chicken nuggets and cereal was now replaced with a strong smell of bleach and rubber.

On March 13, 2020, my teaching career changed forever. When I walked across my university stage to grab my diploma, they told me teachers would have to be flexible. They told me teaching is always changing. They told me to be aware of the technological changes in the global society. I listened, but with wide eyes and an open heart, I was ready to make a mark on the world. I thought the hardest thing that I would have to do would be to break up a fight. Within urban teaching, I knew I would have a few "heart-breaking stories" in my classroom. Nothing prepared me for the heartbreak that overcame when I realized that cold day in March, as I packed my students down with power packs and activity packets, that would be the last time I would see them.

Working in a high need urban school, I am repeatedly being stretched in various ways. I'm on any leadership team that is available to me, I try not to be a 9-5 teacher and try my best to work for my students and families, and I try to make sure that all students have access to my love and kindness. However, I won't lie... when I heard that the Pandemic shut down was going to coincide with our spring break, thus giving us two weeks of a break, I was excited like every other teacher. This year had been especially hard with data collection, new staff personalities, and an overcrowded classroom full of explosive behavior. I was ready for a break, and I was definitely not going to complain about two weeks for a break. Then two weeks turned into "We won't go back until after Easter," ... which then extended to April 31 and finally to we won't be going back. Again, at first, I had no complaints. I was making my own schedule, students texted me if they needed help with the packets. I took the time to learn how to cook with my grandmother, and I spent time on my mental health. Then, 2 weeks had passed. I began to question my purpose and what I was doing to support my students.

I would scroll through Instagram and see all of these teachers working with their students virtually. Teachers sitting in their student's driveways to do read aloud. Teachers even making parades to celebrate the end of the year. I began to notice the inequities in teaching. In undergrad, they tell you that you can make a difference in your students' lives, and you believe them until you get a classroom with outdated computers. You believe them until you're face-to-face with students who have faced trauma from the first day of their life. Despite all of this, I still believed them... until as a district, we passed out thousands of generic packets while other districts and even some schools within my own district opened their online classroom. Let's face it, there is no right way to prepare for a global pandemic. However, the inequities within education definitely showed during this time apart.

I am brought back to the words that stuck with me "We haven't gotten that far." How can we further ourselves as a black community, so a detrimental loss like this does not happen again? During the quarantine time, a few other teachers and I took the time to drive around the community where we worked. There was chaos. Unsupervised children, people were running across the street, almost causing accidents. Abuse. I was heartbroken. The pillar of structure that so many depended on had been taken away, and now what was there?

Moving forward... how can we get further? I would like to share some of my thoughts on what we can do to get further. I would also like to share what I have done in the face of this Pandemic to make it better for my students and parents.

1. Work Together: I realized through all of this that I could not do this alone. I had to rely on my district for help, I relied on my colleagues, and I relied on the parents. We all had to work together. To help us move forward in this, we must continue to work together—yes, teachers, students, and parents must work in tandem.

2. Communicate: Communication is key. It was essential for me during this Pandemic. I knew that my students did not know what to expect, and while I did not know what to expect, I knew that I had to keep the lines of communication open. I decided to check in on my students and parents. I did not hesitate to call them to let them know that I was thinking of them. From my perspective, continuing to communicate with them would make the journey a little easier for us all.

3. Remember my passion: Through this journey, I had to remember my love for teaching. I had to remember my love for the students and why I chose this career. Difficult situations cause us to reflect on our why. This is what kept me going, going back to my why and being dedicated and committed to my passion.

Being an educator during a pandemic has been a challenge, to say the least. However, it has caused us to innovate, develop, and think about things differently. Working together, communicating, and leaning in on my passion has helped me put things properly in perspective... At the end of the day, it is about the students. Our students need me, they need us, and they need us to give them all we got, even amid a pandemic...their education matters!

DORIAN MOORE

Contributing Author

Young and Employed

"Success is a journey, not a destination.
The doing is often more important
than the outcome."
Arthur Ashe

Employment After College

Congratulations, you've just graduated from college! All the studying, 10 plus page papers, and lack of quality sleep have produced a degree. A degree that is supposed to lead a path to gainful employment and a successful career. For a young graduate, finding a job and beginning a career can be difficult. I can attest to this difficulty. As a college-educated woman, I wanted a job that not only provides financial security but recognizes my potential. I went on countless interviews that resulted in the same conclusion, rejection. After receiving a rejection from a job that I really wanted, I requested the employer's feedback on why I didn't get the position. The employer responded with, "You don't have enough experience." Society has told us: Obtain a college degree, and you'll get a good job. In the wake of this final job rejection, I began to realize that having a college degree isn't enough. What no one tells you is that experience lands you the job. Now the question is, how does one gain the experience?

Getting the Experience: Internship vs. Fellowships

The most common way to obtain experience is through internships and/ or fellowships. Internships are defined as a "short-term work experience offered by companies and organizations for students to gain some entry-level exposure to a particular field or industry." Internships are usually completed at the undergraduate level to help students learn about their potential field and gain some skills. Many colleges and universities highlight the importance of completing an internship prior to graduating. Participating in internships while in school can enhance employability by developing hard and soft skills. (Everything You Need to Know About Internships—From What They Are to How to Get One by Lily Zhang)

The benefits of the internship include:

- Opportunity to Explore various career paths within the chosen field of study
- Applying Education in a real word setting
- Develop a Professional Network
- Enhance Professionalism
- Increase Employability

Internship and fellowship are terms that are often used interchangeably, the overall purpose is different. Fellowships are "competitive, short-term funding opportunity for graduate study, scholarly research or professional development." Even though fellowship programs are available at all academic levels, the majority are catered to graduate and post-graduates. Fellowships provide graduates the opportunity to jumpstart their careers. (Profellow)

The benefits of a fellowship include:

- Opportunity to further career
- Receiving Compensation (monetary awards, a living stipend, loan forgiveness, and etc.).
- Additional training and becoming specialized
- Mentorship

My Journey from Young Unemployed New Grad to Gainfully Employed

Taking in the employer's feedback that rejected me, I began the initiative to gain more experience. After what appears as an endless search, the key to kickstarting my career started with an AmeriCorps position posted on Indeed.com. AmeriCorps is "a federal program that places members in intensive service each year to help communities tackle pressing problems while mobilizing millions of volunteers for the organizations they serve." Within AmeriCorps, different programs serve the community in various ways. The program that I applied and did for was MercyServes-Addiction Navigator. The goal of this program was to prevent and reduce opioid abuse in the community. As a MercyServes-Addiction Navigator, I served as a link between emergency department patients who present with substance use issues and addiction services in the community. I chose that particular program because it aligned with my degree, and I recognized the opportunity to enhance my skill set within the healthcare field.

My year of service with AmeriCorps was rigorous, but it provided something that I strived for, which was work experience. Through this work experience, I gained not only skills but the confidence to convey the value of my potential to potential employers. Towards the end of my AmeriCorps service, I resumed the job search and began interviewing. I only went on two interviews, and both employers offered me the position. I said yes to one of the offers, and my career began. Now I'm a gainfully employed young woman who has attained a position that usually takes others years to obtain.

Got the Job, So What's Next?

"Every time you have to make a choice about anything, think, 'Does this go toward or away from what I want?' Always choose what goes toward what you want."
Barbara Sher

Honestly, I don't know what's next. I have a job that I enjoy, that pays well, and lets me have a life. If my father ever found out that I admitted those above, he will likely say to me, "Dorian, you need to have a plan." So maybe that's my next step in formulating a plan for my career. Although I don't have a concrete plan for the next stage of my career, I will continue to look for and seize opportunities. I will continue to make mistakes and learn from them. I will continue to grow professionally. I will continue to work hard and be true.

DAWANNA LEWIS

Contributing Author

Silent Cries for Help

As the ball drops in New York Times Square, "Happy New Year" can be heard throughout the nation. Life as we know it would be anything but normal and happy. The Year 2020 is considered one of the most life-changing years this nation has seen in decades. As the pandemic continues to soar throughout our country, so does the silent cry for help. Mental illness has some of the most serious and deadliest health conditions to date. Why? Because if left untreated, the health condition can kill you and, in some cases, others.

"The strongest people are not those who
show strength in front of the world but
those who fight and win battles that others
do not know anything about"
Jonathan Harnisch.

Mental Illness

Mental illness, defined by Merriam-Webster, states any of a broad range of medical conditions (such as major depression, schizophrenia, obsessive-compulsive disorder, or panic disorder). That is marked primarily by sufficient disorganization of personality, mind, or emotions to impair normal psychological functioning. They cause marked distress or disability and typically associated with a disruption in normal thinking, feeling, mood, behavior, interpersonal interactions, or daily functioning.

Mental illness remains one of the most silent untreated health conditions to date. Discussions about mental illness are considered taboo. As children, we learn to channel our emotions and voices in ways that are not deemed healthy. Imagine being a child making a mistake, being chastised for that mistake only to be told to shut up when expressing pain and sadness. This is only the beginning process of creating an unhealthy mental state? As children, we learn to suffer in silence, those children grow up and become adults who suffer in silence. Adults who never take the time to correct unhealthy learned behaviors as children become a cycle and pattern of bad behavior from generation to generation.

Let's think back to that relative that repeatedly mumbled to themselves, that had sporadic behavior, violent tendencies, and abnormal behavior. How many times did another family member dismiss the untreated behavior with words such as: "Oh he/she are fine," "Don't pay them any attention," "They are harmless," "He/She is crazy," and many other taboo statements. These taboo statement coverups were the silent cries for help. But who was listening?

Mental Illness Causes

So, what causes Mental Illness? Mental illness can be caused by many contributing factors. The following are a few potential causes:

- Genetic Traits
- A chemical imbalance in the brain

- Trauma (Childhood or adult)

- Environmental Stressors

- Drugs and Alcohol

- Stress

- Toxic Relationships

"You are not your illness. You have an individual story to tell. You have a name, a history, a personality. Staying yourself is part of the battle,"
Julian Seifter.

Too Much to Handle

Here we are in the year 2020, living in a pandemic where we have been forced to make quick irrational adjustments. Adjustments, if not made, that are so impactful, could become potentially fatal. This ugly virus has forced everyone to face a new and challenging way of life. It has become a struggle for the minimum task to be completed by the average person. Normal work and school routines are now consolidated. Parents now face multiple roles in a short span of the day while living in fear of the virus.

Government confinements have many people struggling mentally. Now more than ever, people are experiencing the following symptoms (the mayo clinic):

- Feeling sad or down

- Confused thinking or reduced ability to concentrate

- Excessive fears or worries, or extreme feelings of guilt
- Extreme mood changes of highs and lows
- Withdrawal from friends and activities
- Significant tiredness, low energy, or problems sleeping
- Detachment from reality (delusions), paranoia, or hallucinations
- Inability to cope with daily problems or stress
- Trouble understanding and relating to situations and to people
- Problems with alcohol or drug use
- Major changes in eating habits
- Sex drive changes
- Excessive anger, hostility, or violence
- Suicidal thinking

The ability to multi-role an entire household repeated daily has proven to be too much for one person to handle. That normal morning commute time throughout the day no longer exists. The time where one could mentally reset or decompress away from strenuous daily routines no longer exists. Without this time, what should we do?

"Start by doing what's necessary, then do what's possible; and suddenly you

are doing the impossible."
Saint Francis of Assi.

Coping

Even in these challenging times, we need to find ways to help ourselves. Start by listening to your body. The body never lies. Take a nap, drink the water, go for a walk/jog/run in the park, take a drive to nowhere, and woosah. Taking time for you is essentially crucial during this time. Try relaxing activities that allow your brain to reset, bringing back a sense of balance into your life.

Feeling overwhelmed, and the demand is too high? Seek next-level mental health care. Reach out to your doctor, let them know what's going on. There is nothing wrong with treating your mental state. If you are not comfortable in a clinic environment, try talking to someone. Try peer groups where you are free to express yourself without the added taboo pressure. Try talking to a relative or friend. Journalize your thoughts if need be, but find an outlet that will help you cope with the challenging state we live in.

Maybe it's not you that needs the help but someone that you know. As a people, we need to educate ourselves about Mental Illness. Stop frowning down on Mental Illness, but instead try to reduce and minimize the condition by seeking the needed help. Therapy or counseling helps individuals cope with life experiences that are unmanageable as an individual. Understand that it is okay to ask for help. Someone licensed can thoroughly explain what is going on in your life and how you can correct or manage those experiences or situations. If you know someone that needs help or assistance beyond the normal control, meaning they are a threat to themselves or others, seek medical attention through hospitals. If you know someone who needs some additional guidance that may help them get out of a depressed state, seek a licensed counselor for them. Encourage them, walk the journey with them, and let them know they are not alone. There are many agencies with resources to help those at risk for Mental Illness. All it takes is one phone call, and you can help yourself and others.

Concluding this chapter, let's deal with the realities of mental health. No longer will we allow others to silently cry for help. The time is now to seek the needed next-level care. Be caring for relatives, friends, and neighbors. When we see something, we say something. Mental illness is nothing to be ashamed of. An unknown author said, "Your mental health is a priority. Your happiness is essential. Your self-care is a necessity." I challenge each of you to be accountable for self-preservation and the preservation of others. We all deserve to live a life of fulfillment in a manner that is mentally suitable for oneself. Shakespeare said it best, "To thine own self be true." No more silent cries for help.

RAMONA EVANS DANIELS, ESQ.

Contributing Author

LEAP
"Your commitment to step boldly with fearless faith in the face of uncertain times."

In the typical lawyer's office, most expect to walk into a space and immediately see the dark mahogany furniture, computers, legal books, files, framed diplomas, and maybe a bronze statue of lady justice. Not in my office. Each person who enters almost instinctively focuses on a painting of a blindfolded African American woman gracefully stepping forward in the midst of a storm into the safety of the Hand of God. The key point of my intentionally placed piece of art is that she stepped blindly and boldly forward in the storm, not knowing what was next despite her circumstances. That painting has mirrored countless moments in my life where I had a choice to stay in a place of familiarity or step forward blindly with faith even during a storm.

What distinguishes a success story, you see when you scroll through your timeline of a person who overcame insurmountable, unbelievable tragedies or obstacles? Their faith. More specifically, the choices they made based on their faith. My faith rests on my God, my Savior, and His Holy Spirit. Every leap taken in my life was designed by Him and activated by my momentary choice to leap and launch into the unknown.

It doesn't matter if you personally have acknowledged your faith or not; you have it. Whether your faith lies in yourself, someone else, technology, or your God, you have a belief system. Faith is a belief system. Everyone has faith in something or someone. Atheists have faith in the non-existence of God. Agnostics have faith that an unconcerned God watches us from afar. Knowing that whatever you placed your faith in informs your choices every moment, day, week, year, and a decade of your life.

Choices and decisions. Every day we have decisions to make. Sometimes it feels like millions of decisions to make. We decide when we will open our eyes in the morning, slip our feet from the covers, and put our pedicured feet on the floor. We choose whether we will hit the gym, hit the track, or hit the snooze button. Decisions and choices are at our disposal daily. For most of us, the space we are in at this moment is, in large part, a product of our choices. Even when life seems to have been flipped upside down, we still have a choice in how we adjust and respond.

The events that culminated in the late winter/early spring of 2020 were foreseen by few to none of the individuals on planet earth. Yes, catastrophes and unanticipated events are always possible. Still, a worldwide shut down given our technological advances, medical achievements, and faith, did not prevent the health and financial crisis that hit. The coronavirus pandemic of 2020 rudely and swiftly interrupted the regularly scheduled programming of our modern lifestyles. Almost overnight, our daily routines were interrupted, the world itself came seemingly to a screeching halt. The streets were practically empty. We donned masks and savaged stores in an apocalyptic rush to hoard as much antibacterial protection from this unseen virus as we could get our hands-on.

Their true faith and beliefs were made clear for each person in the days and weeks and months that followed. While safe at home/stuck at home, did the visions for your life and future expand or explode? Were you prepared with plans A, B, and C? Where was your faith when the world and lifestyle you knew were stripped away without warning?

For me, my personal and professional lives were both impacted by the pandemic, like most everyone else. Personally, everything from my love of international travel to my weekly routine of worshipping God with praise dance at my local church was disrupted. The source and strength of your faith are tested in how you adjust to disruption. So, instead of exploring the pyramids of Egypt, my husband and I walked the trails and streams near our home on those warm spring days. Instead of dancing barefoot in my white garments before the Lord in the sanctuary, I got my praise on in the middle of my living room. I chose to learn how to meet my emotional, social, and spiritual needs in a new way. Through faith and perseverance, I decided to adjust. When the world stops and your routine is rudely interrupted, chose to learn and adjust.

One of the most powerful and graceful movements for a dancer is the leap. If done skillfully, a leap makes the dancer appear to defy gravity. The dancer, for a moment, is physically overcoming the very laws of gravity and taking flight. In your life, have you been weighed down by your past, your mistakes, your losses? You can choose to stay in that space and limp along or leap forward in the act of faith.

Sounds easy, right? Just kidding. The 'what-ifs' 'I can't' and 'I don't know how's' can be paralyzing for someone not acting in faith. I went from a clientele base of 30 to well over 300 within a year of going into my solo law practice. It wasn't because I had it all figured out, or I was so smart and well-connected in the community- but my God was. See, my faith was not resting on my own shoulders; I put the outcome in His hands. All He wanted was to see me take that first blindfolded step.

What dreams have you deferred? What vision has been put on the back burner because of fear or life's circumstances? What would you do if you knew you wouldn't fail? No, this isn't a perfect time, but isn't it the perfect time to leap? If this pandemic period has shown us anything, it is the unpredictability and brevity of our lives and lifestyles. Never again should the wise among us put off that calling, arrogantly assuming we can do it another time. That elusive 'perfect' time may never come. There are a lot of people who wish they wouldn't have waited for the perfect moment to take that trip of a lifetime, gotten married, or gone to that Essence Fest.

Often the dream is deferred because of a lack of commitment and simple fear. People mistakenly believe others are simply braver or more daring when they leap into the unknown. They're not. The single distinction between the thinker and the doer, the doer, has chosen to 'do it afraid.' There is not a more tragic emotion in life than regret. To look back over your life and see lost opportunities and who you could have been is haunting. Lesson learned. Next time you have a goal, a vision, a dream, don't let it gather dust on a shelf labeled, 'regrets.'

So now that you've decided to live in this life like it's golden and leap, what's next? The bible says to "write the vision and make it plain, so that [s]he may run that read it" Habakkuk 2:2. "Without a vision, the people perish" Proverbs 29:18. Study the vision, know the goal so that it is clear. It's hard to hit a moving target, so next, you have to specifically identify what you want. Once you clearly know what you want to achieve, you should develop an action plan to reach that goal. People often talk a good game about what they want to do without any clue about the work it takes to get there. Successful people chose to put in the work. They 'activate' their faith through work. Like I said earlier, everybody believes in something. Everybody has faith, but the Word says that 'faith without works is dead' James 2:26.

Work may be the act of taking that first step of filling out an application for membership to an exclusive organization you have dreamed of being a part of for years. Work may be auditioning for a role in that local theater. Work may be daily journaling prayers to chronicle your conversations and relationship with God. Work is the bold, uncompromising step in the direction of your goal and vision for that area in your life. Work goes beyond wishes and words, transforming into tangible actions.

Now that you have identified your goal and taken the first step to achieve it by putting in the work be bold. Be intentional. Many dreams never came true because of fear, timidity, and inconsistency. When obstacles come between you and your heart's desire, what is your first instinct? Do you panic, complain, lay blame, quit, or conquer the obstacle by learning to adjust?

My faith tells me that you are too precious to panic, too classy to complain, too much of a leader to lay blame, and too destined to win, so quitting is never an option. The blindfolded woman is me, she is you, and together we are pressing forward with fearless faith until we reach our goal.

SHAHIRA SCHINE

Contributing Author

Black Royalty Clouded by Mental Health

"I wish people could understand that the brain is the most important organ of our body. Just because you can't see mental illness like you could see a broken bone, doesn't mean it's not as detrimental or devastating to a family or individual." ~ *Demi Lovato.*

My grandmother and great-grandfather, who I lovingly called "Big Daddy," were having a huge argument. I had to be 5 or 6 years old, but I remember it like it was yesterday. Some things are fuzzy, but I remember how I felt. They were screaming at the top of their lungs at each other, and he started going after her in near rage. I jumped from fear and shock because I had never seen him so angry. My grandmother was yelling back but I could tell she was starting to get scared. Before I knew it, my great-grandmother who I lovingly called "Big Mama" said "Oh, not with my baby!" and whipped me out that house, into her car and sped like a madwoman so fast, the next thing I knew, we were in church singing "Hallelujah and Praise the Lord!" I felt like I had whiplash. It had to be a night service because it was dark outside. I remember wondering, "How are they are having church at night?" It felt like it happened in 30 seconds; I was so confused. While I didn't understand, it cemented in me, things were not quite right in my home.

As children, loved ones are flawless; as adults, loved ones are human

As a young child, I loved my grandmother, dearly. We had our little secrets I would only tell her. We had our walks on short Vine where everything I asked for received a hard "No!" She taught me how to keep one eye open, and one eye closed, which makes me lovingly think of her every time I put on makeup. When my mom put me on punishment and made me write a phrase 500 times in the middle of summer while my friends played outside, she quickly took the paper and told me to go play and wrote it for me. We would eat watermelon and grapefruit, and she sprinkled salt on it, which I still do this to this very day. I watched her paint her nails and wait for hours for it to dry. I would daydream the day I got older and "did my nails" like her. I watched her do her hair in the kitchen with the hot comb on the stove and wanted my hair to be cute too. She smoked cigarettes, which I HATED, so I had a solo protest outside our house with a poster marching up and down the street. She looked at me from the window, shook her head, and walked away. And even though I hated it, I was curious to see what the big fuss was all about because she did it so much. So, one day I stole a cigarette and lighter from her and snuck down to the basement to try it. I took one puff and coughed and even sneezed so bad I said, "No way!" and never did it again. Only because of her was I curious.

But what I didn't know back then as a young child, my grandmother was taking medicine to control her mental illness. One of the aggravating factors to my great-grandparents is my grandmother never worked; she was never self-sufficient. She never learned how to drive and lived with her parents her whole life. As I'm older, I better understand why my great-grandfather could have been so angry that night. Unfortunately, she gradually started going off her medication. Slowly, she began to slip away from the grandma I knew. Little things changed over time; she stopped doing the things she used to do. She didn't keep her clothes as nice, coordinated, and presentable. She stopped doing her hair and nails as often as she did. The moments we shared began to diminish.

It's hard for children to not see the adults they love as supernatural beings who can do no wrong. But as you grow older, you begin to see them through a different lens with flaws and troubles difficult to overcome. When this happens, you must not love them any less; quite the contrary, love them even more and love them harder. Your love is needed to help them battle through the struggles they endure. The key to reaching this point of understanding is forgiveness. Forgiving them for not being who you thought they were but seeing them for who they really are and loving them anyway. *"Be kind and compassionate to one another, forgiving each other, just as Christ God forgave you." Ephesians 4:32*

Mental Illness Has to Be Addressed, Especially in the Black Family

With my grandma slowly coming off her meds, I saw mental illness take over her. She would have bad dreams and scream through the middle of the night, scaring me. She became angry and hurtful for small reasons or no reason at all. Even more heart-breaking, I started to realize that while she loved me, she didn't give the same loving affection to my mom. She could be cold, distant, and have a sharp tongue with her. I didn't understand until I was much older the contentious relationship they always had. As I grew older, I realized the impact this had on my mother. Understandably, this was extremely hurtful to her. I learned mental illness affected their relationship from the very beginning, and my grandmother was never a mother-figure to my mom. Which is why we were with my great-grandparents; they were the parental figures to my mom and raised her since she was born. But the lack of a mother figure influenced my mom, causing her to be untrusting, feeling unloved, and unwanted. It breaks my heart to realize the hurt my grandmother caused my mother.

A lot of the confusion and hurt can develop when mental health is never discussed. Unfortunately, mental health has traditionally been a dark stigma in the black community. To address it or own, a person suffers from isolation, ridicule, depression, anxiety, stress, and can lead to physical health issues. Awareness and education must constantly be pushed to teach the Black community; there is no shame for anyone suffering from mental health illnesses. When considering the Black community's vast trauma, there is no question of why Black people would be overwhelmed by a wide range of mental health issues. As a community, instead of condemning anyone going through mental health issues, the best solution would be to comfort and empathize with them. Trying to understand their struggles and work to get whatever help is needed. *"Then Jesus said, 'Come to me, all of you who are weary and carry heavy burdens, and I will give you rest.'" Matthew 11:28.*

Lean on Faith to Get Through Uncertainty

When times seem uncertain, confusing, and simply don't make sense, it's best to give it all to God to handle; He has the final say. There were times when I was angry with my grandmother, hurt by her actions, and confused by my mixed emotions on how to feel about her. To get through it, I leaned on my faith to be more understanding. Remembering God is with us always, even when it seems He is not there, He is and is covering you with grace in His own way. Continued faith, even as things do not make sense, seem impossible with no way out, is the force that helps push through to the light at the end of the tunnel. *"The Lord himself goes before you and will be with you; he will never leave you nor forsake you. Do not be afraid; do not be discouraged." Deuteronomy 31:8*

Mental Illness Is a Painful Invisible Wound

This all leads to the opening quote. The mental illness from my grandmother had a detrimental and devastating effect on my family. Causing ripple effects from my mother to me. Ironically, if you met my grandmother and mother today, you would have no idea the combative and emotionally draining relationship they have. My mother is now my grandmother's caretaker and does it lovingly. My mother is bubbly and talkative but deep down inside, still hurting from their painful relationship. My grandmother is now in a frail state and not mentally capable of discussing their issues. The pain caused will never be acknowledged, and there will never be an understanding or apology given. This means the wound will never fully heal. Since my grandmother's mental illness was never deeply diagnosed with counseling or guidance on navigating, it hung like a heavy cloud over my family. It was not an object you could point to as an obvious problem to address but was always there from the day I was born.

Breaking the Stigma of Mental Health

Education on mental health and medical care availability to address it needs to be prioritized in local, state, and federal governments. Education needs to come in numerous forms, from health officials to patients, schools, churches, and, most importantly, at home. Regardless of whether it directly affects a family or not, it needs to be addressed because someone will come across someone else dealing with it in some fashion or another. Teaching it early in the home will help develop sympathy and understanding for anyone who suffers from it. This will help continue an open dialogue on the issues and allow opportunities to end the negative perception typically given.

Stigmas against treating it need to be broken, and more discussions need to be had to heal humanity. Mental health affects people from all backgrounds, ethnicities, and religions. It recently has become a topic due to tragic devastations such as school shootings, police brutality, and a global pandemic due to the coronavirus. This proportionally affects the Black community, hurting our own people even more. The sooner mental health is addressed, the sooner we heal the nation, families from all backgrounds, and especially the Black community and Black families, including mine.

Meet the Authors

Tashawna Thomas Otabil

Tashawna Thomas Otabil currently serves as the Executive Director of Managed Care for TriHealth a $2B Health System in Cincinnati, Ohio. She has nearly 25 years of management experience and proven performance leadership with Managed Care Payer Contracting and Population Health strategies. Tashawna is responsible for contractual relationship management valued at over $1.3 billion dollars in revenue.

Before joining TriHealth, she worked for both payer and provider organizations in various Healthcare leadership and administration roles. Tashawna received a bachelor's degree in Healthcare Business Administration. She always strives for excellence which is evident in her recognitions as of one of Ohio's National Diversity Top 15 Businesswomen (2018), TriHealth Pillar Performance (2018), Healthcare Financial Management Association Bronze Metal (2019) and Leadership awards. In addition to her awards, Tashawna is an Amazon bestselling author of three books, "It Takes Money Honey" (2019), "Leadership Tidbits" (2019) and Leadership Tidbits 2(2020). These publications provide empowerment and strategies to help women excel in their personal and professional endeavors.

Tashawna is committed to public service and is actively involved in the community as a member of the Board of Directors for the Urban League of Greater Southwest Ohio, St. Aloysius organization and the Karen Wellington Foundation. She is also a proud member of Delta Sigma Theta Inc. Lastly, Tashawna is a co-owner of

Black Art Speaks LLC. Black Art Speaks is team of artist that designed and painted the "Black Lives Matter" mural in downtown Cincinnati. She played a very pivotal role in leading and organizing the project which created an opportunity to form an organization. The company focuses on promoting and advocating for artist to share their voice through the power of art while being paid.

CHERYL STALLWORTH LETT

Cheryl Stallworth-Lett is a Sales Director for a leading global Natural & Organic Foods company and a graduate of the University of Cincinnati. A devoted wife and mother, she has been married to Nathaniel Lett, Jr. for 25+ years, and together they parent two adult children, Courtney and Trey.

Shawnda Jo DeRamus, MHA

Shawnda Jo DeRamus is a healthcare administration professional with over 20 years of experience in health economics and finance for leading health systems and medical device companies. She is a proud member of Delta Sigma Theta Incorporated and currently the president of the Cincinnati Alumnae Chapter. She is a devoted super aunt to twin nieces Naomi & Mykal.

DELISHA MURRAY

"Delisha is a woman of God, a wife and a mother who prides herself on inspiring, motivating, and encouraging others to live out their God-given purpose."

Delisha is a native of Detroit, Michigan but moved to Cleveland, Ohio at a very young age. In 2011, Delisha relocated to Cincinnati, Ohio to advance her professional career in the Banking industry.

Prior to moving to Cincinnati, Delisha worked extensively in the nonprofit sector. It is working in this sector that she realized that God had always placed her in leadership positions—many times without the title. Delisha often found herself working as a middle manager navigating through difficult situations in the workplace that often occurred from a lack of leadership, either in role, skillset, or both. In many cases, she became the go-to person who would help resolve organizational issues. Her love and passion to help others advance both within organizations and in life is what led her to pursue a passion that would be birthed in 2015.

In 2015, she started Divine Leadership 365, LLC, a company dedicated to helping improve the lives of others. Through life coaching and leadership development, the goal is to help individuals realize their God given purpose and recognize their leadership potential. The inspiration behind Divine Leadership 365 is God. Delisha operates from the belief that God provides opportunities to lead and these opportunities are all around us—365 days a year.

In addition to life coaching, Delisha enjoys motivational speaking, facilitating and is a certified speaker, teacher and life coach with the John Maxwell Team. Delisha also works in the Banking industry as a Program Officer. She is responsible for coordinating and executing programs and initiatives that impact the Banks Community Reinvestment Act (CRA) Service throughout a 10-state footprint. This includes, but is not limited to, management of a financial empowerment program for high school students, educating 150,000 students per year, and management of the Bank's volunteer management system.

Delisha has doctoral coursework from the University of Phoenix. She obtained a Master of Art in Public Administration from Cleveland State University and a Bachelor of Art in Spanish from Kent State University. Delisha is a proud member of Delta Sigma Theta Sorority, Incorporated.

Delisha and her wonderful husband Charles have three beautiful children, Caylen, Cayla, and Caiyah. Delisha believes that the core of her success has been in large part due to her family—starting with her Dad who nurtured her ambition, her husband, children, siblings, and mother-in-law. Delisha enjoys spending time with her family, reading, writing poetry and living in purpose—everyday.

Amber C. Simpson

Ms. Amber C. Simpson is a native of Cincinnati, Ohio. She is a public school educator with over 20 years of experience. Amber is currently the principal at Pleasant Ridge Montessori School in the Cincinnati Public School District. It is her vision to provide students with the values and learning experiences that will lead to successful careers and contributions to the community at large.

Ms. Simpson has a B.A. in Elementary Education from Kentucky State University located in Frankfort, Kentucky. She received her Montessori ages 9-12 training from Xavier University in Cincinnati, Ohio in 2001. She also has a M.ED in Educational leadership from the University of Cincinnati.

Amber is the proud mother of an amazingly intelligent and talented daughter, Zora Grace. Amber's life is driven by her faith and her family. She is supported and nurtured by a loving immediate and extended family and a close circle of cherished friends. She is a faithful Christian, using her gifts in music, education, and outreach ministries, to support the growth and success of her church, school, and the community. It is her hope that God will be pleased with her labor; "being confident of this very thing, that He who has begun a good work in you will complete it until the day of Jesus Christ." (Philippians 1:6 NKJV)

BRANDI SANDERS

Brandi D. Sanders a contributor to this work of art holds a Master Degree in Business Administration, Master Level Certification in Executive Leadership, she is also a pride member of Delta Sigma Theta Inc.. She has made a career of being a public servant, and has been passionate about serving the community for more than 20 years, in various leadership roles. Her favorite quote is, "With Great Authority comes great Responsibility, and with great Responsibility comes greater Accountability, and with great Accountability comes Humility". Given her experience and work in the community, Ms. Sanders, take the opportunity to advise further leaders of tomorrow, to thy own self be true not allowing their growth and progress to be stunted trying to please or appease others. The best advance Ms. Sanders has received through-out her life is not to lose sight of her goals. Ms. Sanders, has chosen to be a part of this book, because she believes, " to whom much is given much is required!" Hebrews 4:6

JESSICA FRAZIER, M.ED

- Bachelors of Arts, Business Administration, Economics Minor Wilmington College (2004)

- Masters of Education, Educational Leadership, Miami University (2009)

- Licensed Childcare Provider, Hamilton County Job & Family Services & State of Ohio (Jessica's Learning Junction) (Since 2014)

- Licensed Realtor, Hondros College (2018)

Born and raised in Downtown Cincinnati Ohio, Jessica has always been a passionate, energetic and motivated individual. Jessica is a Mother, Realtor, small business owner and God-fearing woman. She is also a newfound author determined to pursue future writing opportunities. This is a woman that is eager, motivated, and enthusiastic about life's never-ending successes and challenges. She's always had a heart for giving back to others and the community. At an early age, she volunteered for the former Laurel Homes community engagements, Aiming High Youth Program iniatives, Downtown Linn Street YMCA programs and events (currently closed), Seven Hills Neighborhood House activities and the Shelterhouse (formally known as the Downtown Drop Inn Center Shelter). Jessica now volunteers at her alma mater Wilmington College in Wilmington, OH with multi-cultural and minority student events, at her church which is located in Downtown Cincinnati, OH, and various other organizations. Jessica is the epitome of a woman of faith as she knows the importance of having faith in the midst of financial hardship. She is not a stranger to life's struggles but has overcome because she chose her faith over her finances. Jessica knows that as long as you rely on your faith, you'll find R.E.S.T. in the midst of any and every trial and tribulation.

Almaz Ware

Almaz Ware was born in Monrovia, Liberia and is a proud Cincinnati, Ohio native. Almaz is an Organizational Development and Training Manager with her bachelor's degree in Psychology and her master's degree in Industrial - Organizational Psychology. Almaz completely lights up when coaching others through their professional journey and finds joy in others reaching their development goals.

Almaz puts God at the center of her life and is actively involved in her Church community. Almaz is happily married to Chad Ware and a devoted mother to 3 beautiful boys: Peyton (10) Brayden (8) and Cairo (1). Almaz is also an active member of Delta Sigma Theta Sorority, Incorporated.

KASI M. JORDAN

Kasi Jordan is a Cincinnati native. She graduated from Walnut Hills High School and went on to pursue a degree in Education. Serving as an elementary school principal, Kasi has worked hard to ensure her students' basic needs are always met. From coordinating coat drives, to sending home "power packs" full of food on the weekends, Kasi has forged strong community partnerships.

Her family has seen the devastating effects drugs have on families as she supports her family by helping to raise 3 children who were left without parents. This unexpected circumstance pushed her to speak out in an attempt to educate others on how to raise children who have experienced trauma. Often described as a life-long learner, Kasi has committed herself to support those who don't always have a voice.

Kasi is the proud mother of a son, Darryn and a daughter, Kamryn and a member of Delta Sigma Theta Sorority, Incorporated.

SHEVA STEPHENS

Sheva S. Stephens is an ordained Pastor serving as the West Campus Pastor of the City of Promise Church. A current student of Northern Theological Seminary in pursuit of a Master of Divinity with a concentration in New Testament Studies; her faith and trust in God is often on full display. Having completed her secular studies with a Master of Science from Syracuse University Whitman School of Business in Professional Accounting, she answered "The Call" to pursue additional knowledge. This calling honors a foundation of speaking to God's people on God's behalf. Sheva's heart for inviting anyone into the knowledge of Jesus and His healing, soul saving, empowering knowledge oozes from her speech and any encounter that you may have with her. Sheva is joined to her childhood sweetheart and with their blended family, parent two daughters and one son. Given one moment to speak with Sheva and you will know that family is everything to her. Any endeavor that she embarks upon us predicated with a thought towards how it may empower, enrich, and grow her children and eight grandchildren. What will I do with my dash? I will honor God with my dash.

BEVERLY ENGRAM

Beverly A. Engram is retiring after 35 years as a public servant with the City of Cincinnati, where she led the financial operations for one of the 17 city departments. Early in her career, she began fighting for employee rights where she held leadership positions in the local labor union organizations, the American Federation of State County and Municipal Employees (AFSCME), City's Middle Management Association, and Cincinnati Organized and Dedicated Employees (CODE). She served on teams to negotiate labor management agreements and ensured employees received honest and fair treatment during disciplinary actions. She also led youth mentoring programs graduating over 300 of Cincinnati's students and continues to mentor and tutor today. She loves spending time with her friends and family, enjoys bowling and participating in the Heart Mini Marathon 5k and 9k races, the Flying Pig Half Marathon and the Queen Bee Half Marathon and 4k races and working in the community.

Beverly is a graduate of the Northern Kentucky University where she earned a B.S. in Finance and Business Administration.

Beverly is married to her husband Rodney for over forty years, has 2 adult daughters (both who are employees of the City of Cincinnati as well), and 3 grandchildren. She is a member of the Corinthian Baptist Church where she serves on the Usher Board and a member of Delta Sigma Theta Sorority, incorporated.

TIFFANEY HARDY

Ms. Tiffaney J Hardy is a 16-year public servant with the City of Cincinnati known for her hard work and dedication. She has diverse leadership experiences with both the public and private sector. As the Assistant Treatment Superintendent of Media and Marketing for Greater Cincinnati Water Works (GCWW), she is responsible for internal and external communications, brand development, marketing, media relations, social media outreach, risk communications as well as developing community engagement strategies and programming for diverse stakeholders.

Tiffaney is a 2018 Emmy winner as an Executive Producer for the community relations video 'Juncta Juvant' and for the Emmy-nominated "The PivotPoint' Documentary in conjunction with Cincinnati Police Chief Eliot Isaac, the Cincinnati Police Department, and ZoMotion Pictures.

She is a graduate of the University of Cincinnati with Bachelor of Arts Degree with honors as a Dean's List recipient and McMicken College of Arts & Sciences Commencement Speaker for the Class of 2000. She earned her Masters of Community Planning degree from the University of Cincinnati College of Design, Architecture, Art, and Planning in 2002. In 2019, Tiffaney completed her Masters of Business in Executive Leadership and Organizational Change with honors from Northern Kentucky University.

In 2000 she was appointed to serve on the Cincinnati Board Health as a member and youngest

221

chairperson of the Cincinnati Board of Health dealing with many public health, water quality, and environmental justice issues.

Tiffaney is a proud member of the Cincinnati Alumnae Chapter of Delta Sigma Theta Sorority, Inc.

She enjoys reading, fishing, boating, experiencing nature, listening to music, and is a sports enthusiast.

LEAH STEWART

Leah Alexander-Stewart was born into a family of educators. She is the youngest, having one older sister, Anittra Alexander. Both her late father, Jackie Alexander and her mother Mable Alexander, dedicated their lives to teaching in P-12 public school systems. Therefore, it came natural for her to also become an educator. She is a higher education professional of over 30 years, having experience working at a research 1 university, a small private university and she is currently employed at a 4-yr comprehensive university where she holds the title of Assistant Vice President for Enrollment and Financial Aid.

As AVP for Enrollment and Financial Assistance, Alexander-Stewart takes great pride in her work. She is known on college campuses as an administrator who goes beyond the call of duty. Leah is a member of local, state and national professional higher education associations. She also serves on numerous campus committees. Through her work and dedication, she has always been a true advocate for students.

Alexander-Stewart stands firm on her philosophical view of education. She believes that college should be available to every individual interested in pursuing a formal or advanced education beyond high school. However, she also understands that there are barriers and inequalities, which prohibits people from attending college. Her mission is to break addition to her commitment and dedication to her work, she also volunteers countless hours to committed service to the African American community.

Her involvement with Envision Children was one of her most engaging and memorable service opportunities. Leah served on the Board of Envision Children, it is a nonprofit education services provider targeted towards under-served students with the focus on math, technology, science, reading and critical thinking. It provided Leah with the opportunity to give back and it aligned with her philosophical view on education. She continues to be engaged in the community but field a need to call out Envision because it remains near and dear to her heart.

As a mother of three, Leah enjoys being involved in her daughter's lives, Jalyn, Jordyn and Jada who she affectionately calls her J3 Squad. Her children also live by her educational views. Jalyn and Jordyn have demonstrated high academic achievement as college students, studying Civil Engineering and Nursing, respectively and Jada just entered her first year of high school, she too is an honor student.

IVORY PATTERSON

Ivory Patterson is from Milwaukee, Wisconsin and is a member of Delta Sigma Theta Sorority, Inc. She received her Bachelor of Science degree in Biochemistry from Hampton University in 2013 and went on to earn her Dual Master of Health Administration and Public Administration from The Ohio State University in May 2017. She has dedicated her life and career to improving the health of her community by working to reduce health disparities. She believes that everyone should have an equitable opportunity to achieve their best possible health. She also serves as the 2020-2021 Civic Engagement Committee Chair for the Urban League Young Professionals. Here, she develops voter education programming focused on encouraging under-represented communities to exercise their right to vote. In her free time, she enjoys spending time with her friends, creating new tea blends, and trying new recipes.

Sherry L. Whitlock, MS, BS, MT

Sherry L. Whitlock has been described as one who "does not settle for mediocrity", and she lives up to this standard.

After graduating from Wilmington College (Ohio) and Providence Hospital School of Clinical Laboratory Science in 1990, Sherry continued her education at the University of Cincinnati where she received a Masters degree in Healthcare Administration and Planning. She was immediately recruited by Findlay Street Neighborhood house to manage a community health education program in partnership with the Cincinnati Health Department. After leaving Findlay Street, Sherry held several healthcare positions within the Cincinnati area, and eventually landed at Cincinnati Bell Telephone where she worked as a Community Relations Associate.

Having determined in which direction her life should take her and following her dream, Sherry eventually jumped into the real estate arena. She purchased the initial rental property in March 2001, and after purchasing several more, she incorporated and became known as The Principle Group, LLC.

After many years of success in the residential rental business, Sherry began contemplating the idea of heightening her real estate career. In 2018 she started Masterpiece Properties, LLC, a residential rehabilitation corporation. And in 2020 Masterpiece Construction, LLC came to fruition.

Sherry currently serves on the Board of Directors of Queen City Foundation and is a past member of the St. Xavier High School PAC Executive Board. She is also an active member of Delta Sigma Theta Sorority, Inc, Jack and Jill of America, Inc. and Impact100.

PATRICE MATTHEWS

Patrice Finley Matthews is an Account Revenue Specialist for Ensemble Health Partners. Employed for over 1 year collecting from Insurance companies on behalf of the patient for the benefit of recovering funds for area Mercy Hospitals. Prior to this Patrice spent the majority of her career in Retail Banking working as a Relationship Manager for Provident Bank & Key Bank. Patrice was born in Birmingham, Alabama and attended Spelman College in Atlanta , Georgia where she received a Bachelor of Arts in Economics with a minor in Marketing. Patrice has spent 25 years here in Cincinnati, where she discovered her passion in fitness as a Zumba instructor in 2011. Following her passion in dance helped to sustain an additional link to family that help with fitness and nutritional goals. Patrice has worked in Fitness teaching Zumba, Silver Sneakers and Aqua Zumba at Fitworks & Powell Crosley YMCA. Patrice is married with 2 adult children

RETINA M. CARTER

Retina M Carter is a corporate professional at Procter & Gamble, wife, and mother of four beautiful children.

A seasoned professional at Procter & Gamble (P&G), 18 years of supply chain, manufacturing, and product innovation experience developed her strategic leadership and collaboration skills. These skills led to outstanding performance evaluations, numerous corporate awards, including the CEO Award, and even a special assignment in an "Executive-On-Loan" experience to the National Underground Railroad Freedom Center and Cincinnati Museum Center. In addition to delivering strong results individually, Retina holds a passion for coaching others to success in their career journeys.

A dedicated servant of her community, Retina has volunteered with the United Way of Greater Cincinnati for the past 14 years. A member of several leadership giving societies, she ascended to the Chair position for the Herbert R Brown Society of United Way. In this position, she oversees the engagements of donors, volunteer activities, and strategic involvement with United Way leadership. As well, Retina was one of the United Way Champions of Change who designed and executed the 1st time ever, 2020 Black Empowerment Works Grants Program. This program raised and dispensed $600,000 to grassroots organizations dedicated to uplifting the community.

Seeing the youth of the local area succeed is a heart-driven passion for this mother of four children. Retina is the leader of the Procter & Gamble Adopt A Class program. Under her leadership, each school year, over 100 volunteers engage across several Cincinnati Public School classes to provide monthly class activity sessions, mentoring & guidance, and a finale class trips to remember.

A native of Chicago, IL, Retina earned her B.S. Electrical Engineering from Southern Illinois University-Carbondale and is a licensed Project Management Professional. Retina is member of Delta Sigma Theta Sorority, Inc. Her personal motto in life is to "leave an imprint that makes an impact".

DIANNA L. PLEASANT

Dianna Pleasant has 19 years of teaching experience with Cincinnati Public Schools. She has earned a Master's Degree of Education in Multicultural Literature from Xavier University, Cincinnati, Ohio, and a Bachelor's of Science Degree in Education with a Minor in Special Education from Miami University, Oxford, Ohio. She has obtained endorsements in Montessori Education, and Gifted and Talented Intervention. Dianna completed the Teachers Leadership Program (TLP) through Cincinnati Federation for Teachers, and is currently the union building representative for her school. She serves on the instructional leadership team, and has served in many other leadership positions throughout her teaching career with CPS. Dianna is also a proud and active member of the Cincinnati Alumnae Chapter of Delta Sigma Theta Sorority, Inc.

Dianna has a true passion for traveling. She organizes multiple and enjoyable trips each year with close family and friends; to explore the culture, architecture, language and foods of other people around the world. Dianna believes that meeting people from diverse backgrounds is the most rewarding part about traveling, because it helps build her knowledge about different cultures, and shapes her experiences with others.

KIRSTEN L. VAN KALLEN HAMPTON

Kirsten L. Van Kallen Hampton is a Speech-Language Pathologist in the Greater Cincinnati area where she works with middle and high school students to improve their communication skills in order to be effective communicators in the academic setting and their community. Born and raised in Los Angeles, CA; Kirsten received a Bachelor of Arts degree in Communication Disorders and Sciences from California State University, Northridge. She went on to receive her Master of Arts degree in Communication Sciences and Disorders from Hampton University in Hampton, VA.

Kirsten is a progressive leader with a desire to provide mentorship to African American youth and volunteer within communities to improve the lives of its residents, especially those individuals that are often forgotten. She currently serves on the executive board for the Urban League Young Professionals of Greater Southwestern Ohio as the Vice President. She is a also a proud member of Delta Sigma Theta Incorporated. In addition, she volunteers with Envision Children, a non-profit education service provider. In her free time, Kirsten loves to travel, read, and advocate for lupus awareness.

DANIELLE BATTLE

Danielle Lynn Battle serves as an assistant principal at Withrow High School, Cincinnati, Ohio.

Prior professional work experiences include holding positions as a science teacher at Western Hills High School and Hughes STEM High School, and Gear-Up academic tutor at the University of Cincinnati.

Ms. Battle attended McAuley High School, Cincinnati Ohio. Upon graduation from high school she received a scholarship to Wright State University, Dayton, Ohio.

Ms. Battle has a B.A. in Psychology from Wright State University, Dayton, Ohio. a M.Ed. in education from Xavier University, Cincinnati, Ohio.

Ms. Battle is credentialed and licensed by the State of Ohio in Secondary School Administration and certified to teach biological science courses.

Civic involvement is a key aspect of Danielle Battle's background and experiences. She participated in Cincinnati Enquirer's 2001 Neighbor to Neighbor committee which laid the groundwork for people from Cincinnati's 52 neighborhoods to engage in deliberative conversations about Race Relations. She created opportunities in community settings for youth to experience how their voices might be heard by deliberating about the Achievement Gap.

As a teacher she was on the forefront of efforts that involved collaboration and partnership with community businesses and organizations. One significant project was working with corporate executives of Macy's Department Stores to provide students with beyond the classroom learning experiences.

Danielle Lynn Battle is a proud member of Delta Sigma Theta Sorority, Incorporated and the daughter of James C. Battle and Dorothy E. Battle Ph.D.

TAMMY L. SOLOMON-GRAY

Tammy L. Solomon-Gray, M.Ed. was educated in the Cincinnati Public Schools system. After graduating from Aiken Senior High School, she became interested in K-12 education while earning a Bachelor of Arts in African American Studies at the University of Cincinnati. During her work with high school students in UC's Upward Bound Program, it became clear to Tammy that she could make a bigger impact in elementary education.

The second semester of her senior year in college, she was diagnosed with Relapsing-Remitting Multiple Sclerosis, an auto-immune disease of the central nervous system for which, yet, there is no cure. Surrounded by a huge and loving village of family and friends, Tammy went on to earn not one but two master's degrees in Elementary Education and Education Administration from Xavier University and UC respectively. In 2002, she was the subject of an Essence magazine article entitled, "The Courage to Heal: Inspiring stories of three extraordinary women who battled illness-and won." In 2003, Tammy was tapped as a YWCA Career Women of Achievement Rising Star.

Tammy's service as an educator began with three years of experience as a paraprofessional and cheerleading coach in the 1990's. Her nine years in the classroom were in Princeton City Schools, at the Alliance Academy, and in the Lakota Local Schools. In 2009, Tammy's dream was fulfilled as she returned to CPS to serve as an assistant principal at Pleasant Hill Academy and Cheviot-Gifted Academy, West.

Tammy has been Principal and Leader of Leaders at Cheviot School-Gifted Academy, West for 11 years. She has developed a culture of collective leadership in all stakeholders, staff, and students. In 2016, "Leadership for all" resulted in Cheviot School receiving one of the first Momentum Awards from the Ohio Board of Education which recognizes districts and schools for exceeding expectations in student growth for the year. Another proud achievement for her is Cheviot School becoming the first Franklin-Covey Leader in Me school in southwest Ohio. Last year, Cheviot earned its prestigious "Lighthouse Leader in Me School" designation.

Tammy is married to her husband, Mason, she has a son and daughter-in-law, Michael Jamal and Caitlin, and she is also a grandmother of Grayson and Charli. She serves as an MS Advocate, an MS Walk Captain for her own team TSG, and as a National MS Society-Ohio Board of Trustees member.

CARA OWSLEY

Cara Owsley is the director of photography and photojournalist at the Cincinnati Enquirer. Cara has been on staff at the Enquirer for 15 years. Prior to working for The Enquirer, she was a staff photojournalist at The Times-Picayune in New Orleans, The Sun Herald in Biloxi, Mississippi, and The Repository in Canton, Ohio. The Louisville, Ky. native has a bachelor's degree in photojournalism from Western Kentucky University.

In 2018 The Cincinnati Enquirer won a Pulitzer Prize in the local reporting category. The story "Seven Days of Heroin" was recognized by the Pulitzer board "for a riveting and insightful narrative and video documenting seven days of greater Cincinnati's heroin epidemic, revealing how the deadly addiction has ravaged families and communities." Owsley was a photojournalist and photo editor for the project.

Owsley is a single mother with one daughter who is a junior at Indiana University- Purdue University at Indianapolis. Owsley is a member of the Cincinnati Alumnae Chapter of Delta Sigma Theta, Inc., a board member of the Greater Cincinnati Pro Chapter Society of Professional Journalists and serves on the board of the Visual Task Force with the National Association of Black Journalists.

CARRITA A. HIGHTOWER, PhD

Dr. Carrita A. Hightower is an experienced Senior Scientist for a Fortune 100 consumer goods company. She is a proud native of Memphis, TN with a love for southern cuisine. She holds degrees in Human Nutrition/Sensory Analysis from Tennessee State University (BS) and Kansas State University (MS/PhD). Dr. Hightower has been recognized for scientific excellence with multiple US patents and publications in peer reviewed research journals. She has a passion for learning as she considers herself both a research scientist and a teacher- living by the quote "Let the Love of Learning Rule Humanity." She believes in servant leadership and enjoys working with students to improve core academic skills such as reading. Dr. Hightower is a proud member of Delta Sigma Theta Sorority, Incorporated, enjoys traveling, and spending time with family and friends.

Kamyia Fletcher

Kamyia Fletcher is a 25 year old graduate student from Cincinnati, OH. She is best known for teaching 2nd grade. She is also a graduate student at Miami University. Studying transformative education in language and literacy, she seeks to find ways to bring education forward to the future for ALL black and brown students through literacy. She enjoys ice cream...as should all right thinking people. She also enjoys collecting picture books, traveling, and exploring new restaurants.

DORIAN MOORE

Dorian Moore is a licensed social worker who believes in empowering others and making a positive impact in their lives. Ms. Moore holds a bachelor's degree in Social Work from Northern Kentucky University and a MSW from the University of Cincinnati. She's a proud AmeriCorps alumna and will continue to serve those in the community. Her leisure activities include traveling, running, experiencing new restaurants, and spending time with loved ones.

Dawanna Lewis

Dawanna Lewis holds a Bachelor Degree in Financial Management and Planning and a Master of Business Administration. She has worked in the financial branch of the United States Government for over 20 years. Ms. Lewis certificates include Lean Six Sigma, Enhanced Defense Financial Management and Certified Financial Management Certificate Level II.

Ms. Lewis co-founded Girlfriends Giving Back in 2012. Girlfriends Giving Back is a non-profit organization advocating for the hungry and displaced. Ms. Lewis has a passion for her community youth and remains active in the community. Ms. Lewis is a World Double Dutch Champion and has coached a World winning Double Dutch Team.

Ramona Evans Daniels, Esquire

Attorney Ramona Evans Daniels, a Cincinnati native, pursued higher education on the campus of the Ohio State University, in Columbus. At the Ohio State University, she earned a bachelor's degree in Journalism and a double major in Women's Studies and African American Studies. After graduation from the University of Cincinnati College of Law and successfully passing the bar exam, Ramona quickly established a reputation as a fierce and focused litigator in the areas of family law and criminal defense.

In addition to pursuing justice for her clients in the legal field, Ramona has consistently served each community she has lived in with her time and compassion. She is also a proud member of Delta Sigma Theta Incorporated.

Ramona has been married to her high school sweetheart, Marc for more than 20 years. They enjoy travel, fitness and time with good friends, family, and food. They have been blessed with two children, Kayla, and Joshua Daniels.